C0-GDD-863

Franz Gertsch   Seasons

FRANZ GERTSCH

SEASONS Works 1983 to 2011

KUNSTHAUS ZÜRICH

KERBER ART

Contents

FOREWORD

For many years now, Franz Gertsch has been a well-known artist at the Kunsthaus Zürich. It is not only generations of school children who have memorised the works of his featured in our collection – works which, in many cases, were the viewer's very first connection to the visual arts. Gertsch's naturalism tends to fascinate people, and they instantly grasp what he is about: the quiet, seemingly withdrawn figures, the still-life-like pictures of vegetation and landscapes, the painting and prints in the subtlest shades of colour and light. Nothing is left to chance; everything is artistic, and nothing artificial.

Gertsch possesses extraordinary technical skills, which he has consistently honed since the beginnings of his exploration into pop art. Even when representational, painting is capable of more than any other medium – at least when it is practised with such perfection, and when it avoids complacency. Good craftsmanship doesn't make a song and dance about itself. It best celebrates its source when it is the means to an end. The perfectly painted pictures of Franz Gertsch are neither likenesses nor alternative worlds; they diffuse into the everyday reality of the viewer, cautiously but unmistakeably. Casually speaking, one might say that they make their mark, and have been doing so for many decades, without noticeably dating or growing old-fashioned – probably since they are less concerned with the momentary fleeting event than with a specific state. Art is not timeless. Nevertheless, it is to Gertsch's credit that his art has staying power precisely because it makes no promises that it cannot keep. Over the past four years, with characteristic tenacity, he has created a magnum opus, the culmination of his oeuvre to date: the quartet of monumental landscape paintings on the four seasons, which will now occupy the spotlight for the first time in their entirety. Both the artist and the museum have waited for this moment with bated breath. Choosing the seasons as a theme was a wise move, as the quartet itself becomes a cycle of recurring nature and changing settings, which time and again fill observant viewers with amazement. Ultimately there is not conclusion but renewal – and what else can spur on an artist's activity? This is a demanding project to which we have dedicated ourselves, with anticipation, for years. It has been reassuring to know that Swiss Re was at our side offering generous support as a Partner for contemporary art – for which we sincerely thank all those involved, including the Board and Management and, above all, Anne Keller and Diana Pavlicek for their invaluable cooperation.

The main focus of the exhibition is on the new 'Seasons' cycle. To complement it, Tobia Bezzola, the curator of the exhibition, cooperated with Gertsch in selecting a number of earlier works which, taken as a whole, form a high-density composition – and as in a canon yield, as it were, a single picture. Our thanks also go to the Kunsthaus team, in particular to Sandra Haldi for her professional organisation of the exhibition and the editorial tasks she has undertaken; to our Museum technicians, as well as the Registry, Restoration and Press and Communication departments; and to the Education Department programme. Seldom in the more-than-fifty-year history of the museum have works of art created such a harmonious impression in the vast spaces of the exhibition hall – and how few artists there actually are who are capable of achieving this! Franz Gertsch, a guest exhibitor at the Kunsthaus Zürich for the second time, can once again accept this compliment for himself. We join our visitors in extending our warmest thanks to him and his wife Maria for both the exhibition and this book.

Christoph Becker

MESSAGE FROM THE SPONSOR

Eternity and the moment are the signature themes in the work of Franz Gertsch. For four decades now, the artist has surprised us with an opus in which the fleeting present is consolidated into something enduring. Gertsch achieved his international breakthrough with his colossal paintings based on photographic artwork, with which he created icons for an entire age. With his woodcuts, he opened up new dimensions in the world of art. It says something about the importance of Gertsch that the monumental nature of his opus never serves to intimidate the viewer. Quite the contrary: when viewed from afar, his works suggest an uncanny degree of precision, while up close they fragment into purely pictorial or graphic details, thus creating an experience that touches upon the secret of human existence. Possibly, the meaning of life is also only revealed from a certain distance.

With this exhibition, Kunsthaus Zürich offers a comprehensive overview of Franz Gertsch's work from the last thirty years. With the 'four seasons' paintings, the Museum also presents the four-part monumental painting cycle completed only recently by the artist. Taken as a whole his artistic creation can be understood as a sequence of defined conceptual seasons. To grasp this at a sensory level is part of the pleasurable experience of the Zurich exhibition.

The large format of Gertsch's works militates against their global availability. To survive a change of location unscathed, they must be taken out of their frames – always a tricky business. Therefore a Gertsch exhibition is always a singular event, and a unique opportunity to get to know or rediscover one of the most important contemporary Swiss artists. As the reinsurer, Swiss Re is particularly pleased to have assisted in making this exhibition of Franz Gertsch's works possible. As a Partner for contemporary art, we hope that all those interested in the fine arts will find their stroll through the 'Seasons' a stimulating and inspiring experience.

Swiss Re – Partner for contemporary art

FACES AND LANDSCAPES: ALL IN A DAY'S (ART)WORK FOR FRANZ GERTSCH

Like a house painter perched high up on some scaffolding who, hour after hour, brushstroke by brushstroke, accomplishes his day's work – sometimes no more than a few square centimetres – with an air of calm, patient discipline: this is not how the public envisions an artist.

The public prefers its painting genius intoxicated, explosive and febrile. This has been the case since the days of the first Van Gogh craze, and it can still be seen in the veneration of Modigliani, Pollock, Bacon, Polke and Basquiat, to name but a few.

But what about someone who, as a young artist, didn't feel like going into a trance? In the late 1950s, you could at best construct painting machines to mock the daubs of the intoxicated genius. Or you could tear down posters from walls and create collages, or cut out newspaper photos and take them straight to the machines in the silk-screen print studio.

These were, in a nutshell, the artistic fronts that the young Franz Gertsch found himself facing. His generational companions either followed the expressive tradition and turned to impulsive gestures, or cast their lot with the Nouveau Réalisme camp. One could fall, without trace, into the no-man's-land between these two approaches. Neither Arnold Rüdlinger's *Tendances actuelles 3* (1955, with Michaux, Wols, Tobey and Pollock) nor the subsequent burgeoning neo-dadaism of the Tinguely clique offered a suitable lifeline to the artistic tendencies of the young Gertsch in 1950s Bern, however. Gertsch wasn't part of the scene – he was never really part of the scene anywhere – and he refrained from cheap corroboration.

Since then, for the last five decades, Franz Gertsch has worked unencumbered by the fashions of salons and biennials. At times, coincidentally, he has crossed paths with the trendsetters (for example, in *documenta 5*), after which he seemed to distance himself from them once again. This has made no difference as far as Gertsch's art is concerned. Unlike his celebrated German colleagues, he has never flirted with meta-painting. His art does not speak of how it stands up to other art, nor does it speak of how other art stands up to *it*. Neither does it complain that real painting has died out or can be expected only in the distant future.

Gertsch's art is the thing itself. It, too, does not examine how it stands up to these faces and landscapes; rather, it examines how the faces and landscapes stand up to *it*. Or in Gertsch's own words: 'I've chosen the radical path – reality as painting.'

Tobia Bezzola

Gräser I (Grass I), 1995/96
Mineral pigments (bound in damar resin and
beeswax) on unprimed cotton canvas, 240 x 340 cm
museum franz gertsch, Burgdorf

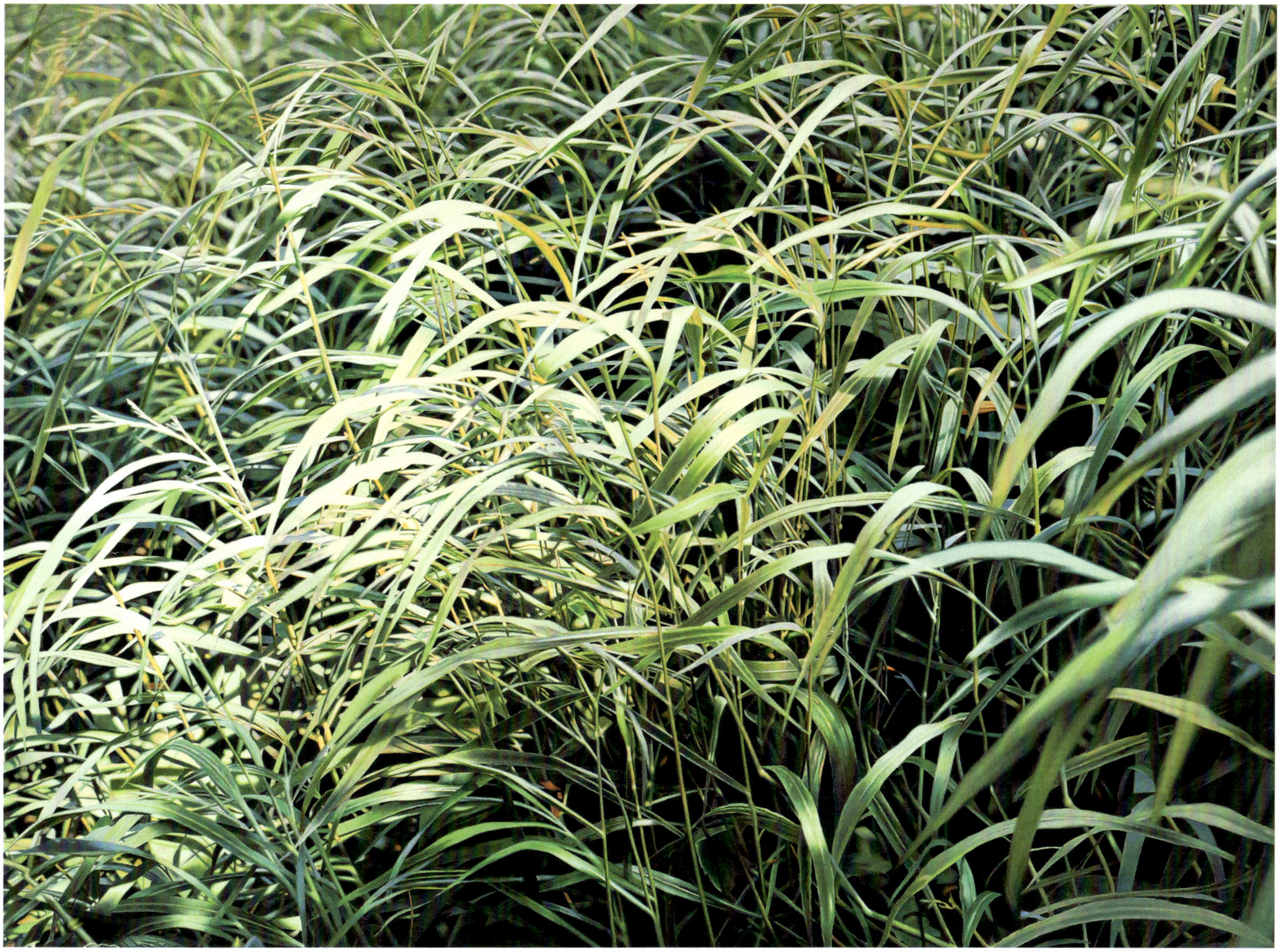

Gräser II (Grass II), 1996/97
Mineral pigments (bound in damar resin and beeswax) on unprimed cotton canvas, 290 x 290 cm
museum franz gertsch, Burgdorf

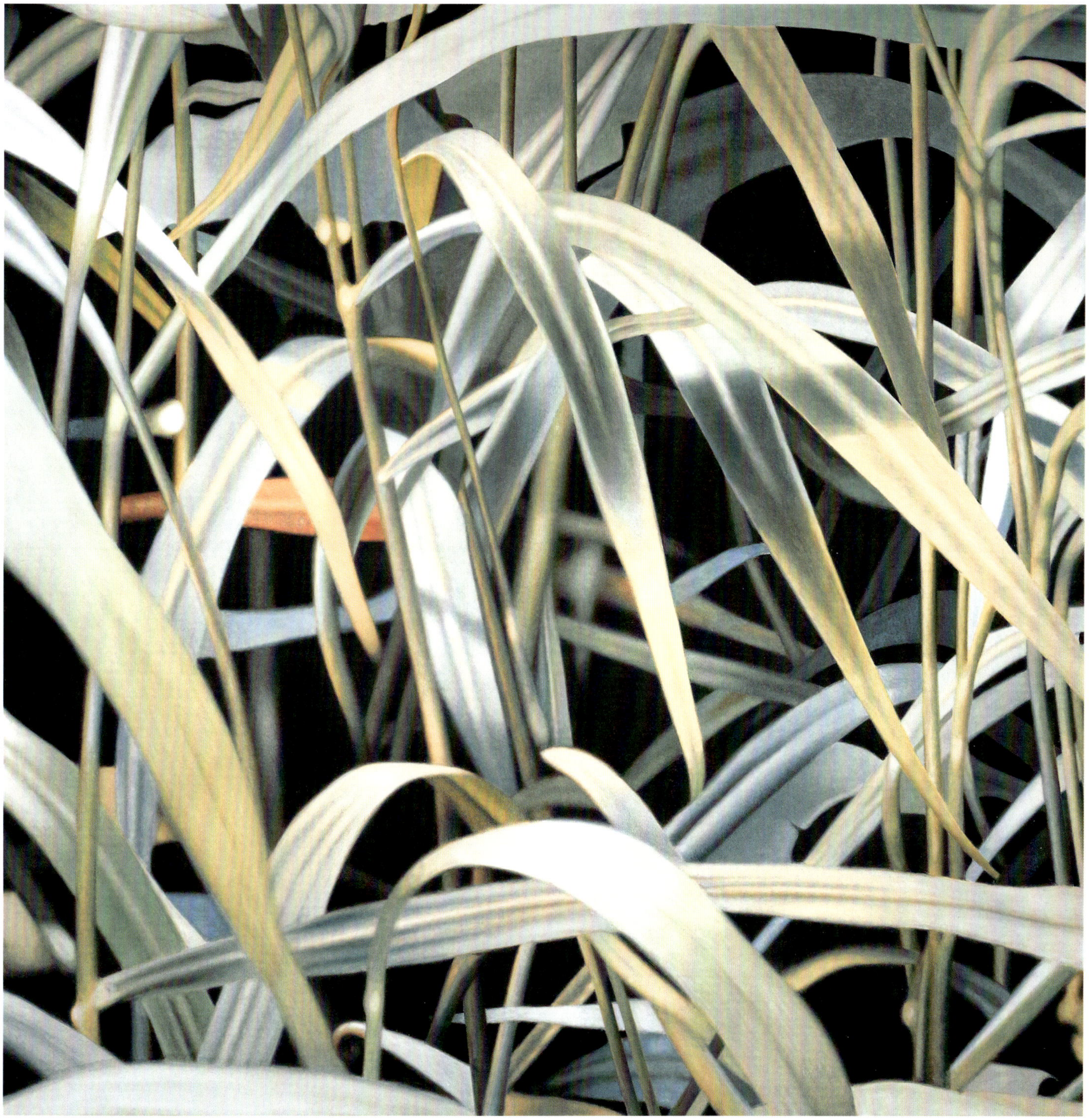

Gräser III (Grass III), 1997
Mineral pigments (bound in damar resin and beeswax)
on unprimed cotton canvas, 290 x 290 cm
museum franz gertsch, Burgdorf

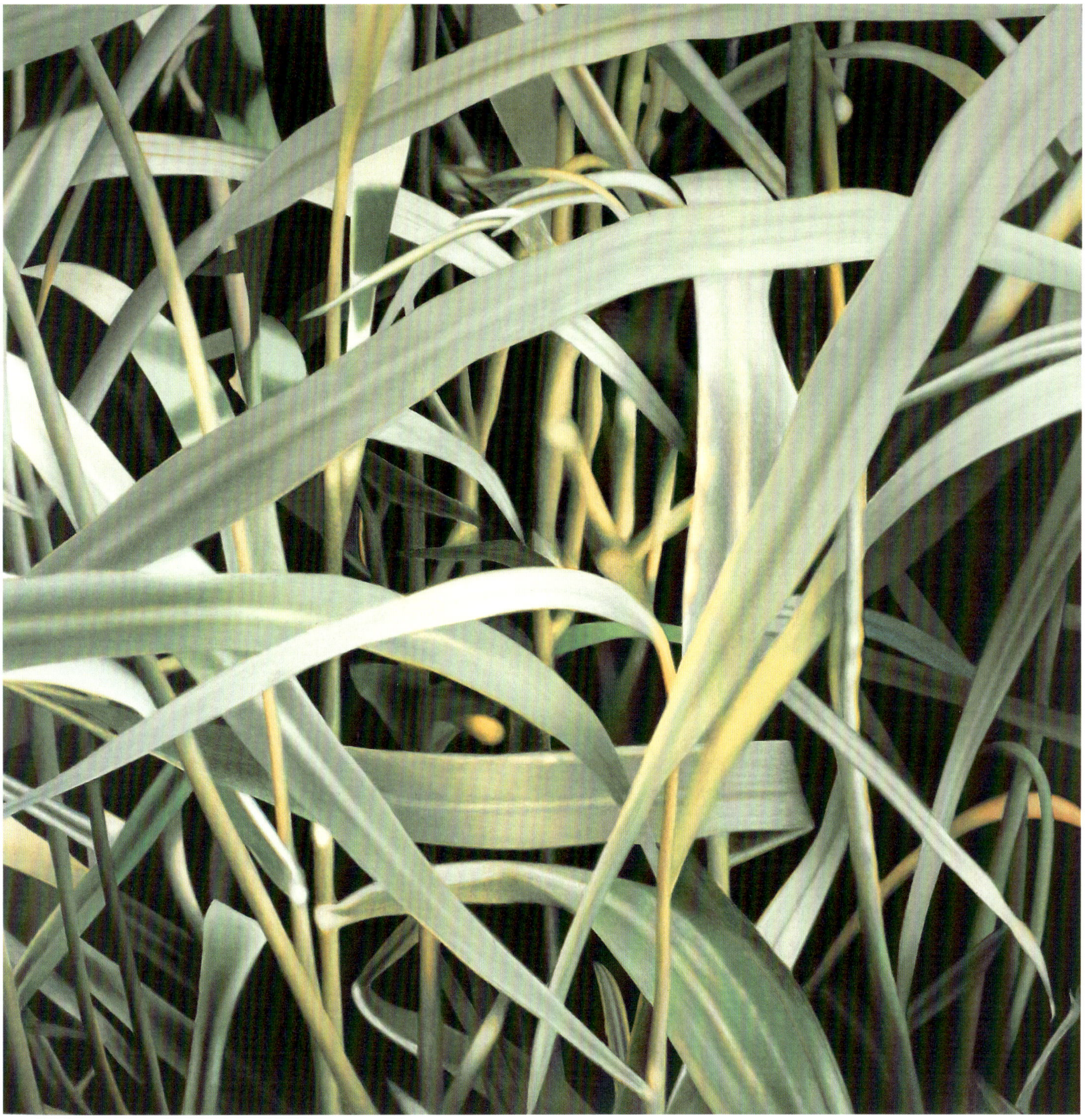

Gräser "Ausblick" (Grass 'Prospect'), 2007
Woodcut (2 plates), 268 x 183 cm each
Hand-pulled print no. 7 on Kumohadamashi Japan paper
made by Heizaburo Ivano, 276 x 380 cm. Lapis lazuli
Collection of the artist

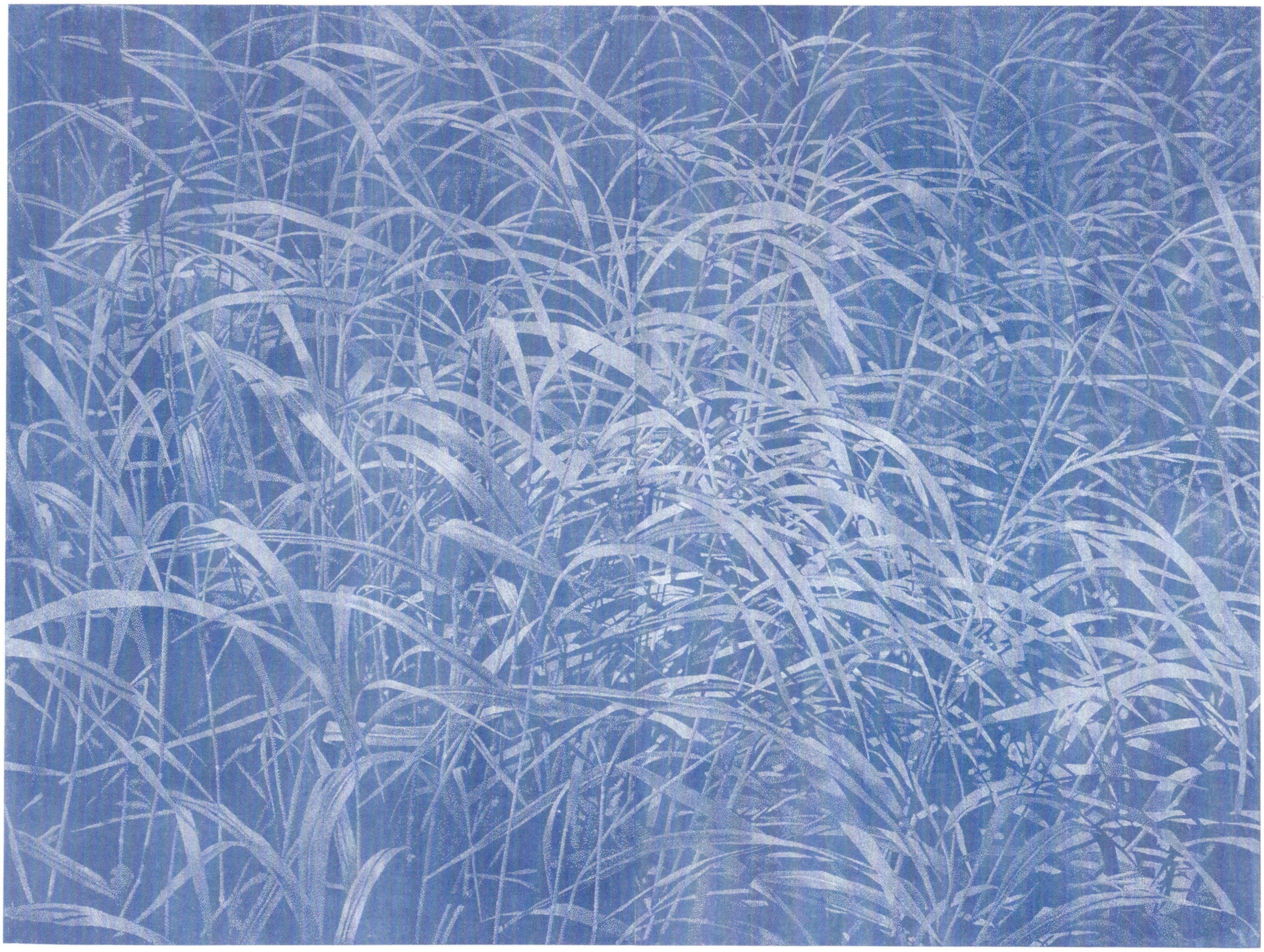

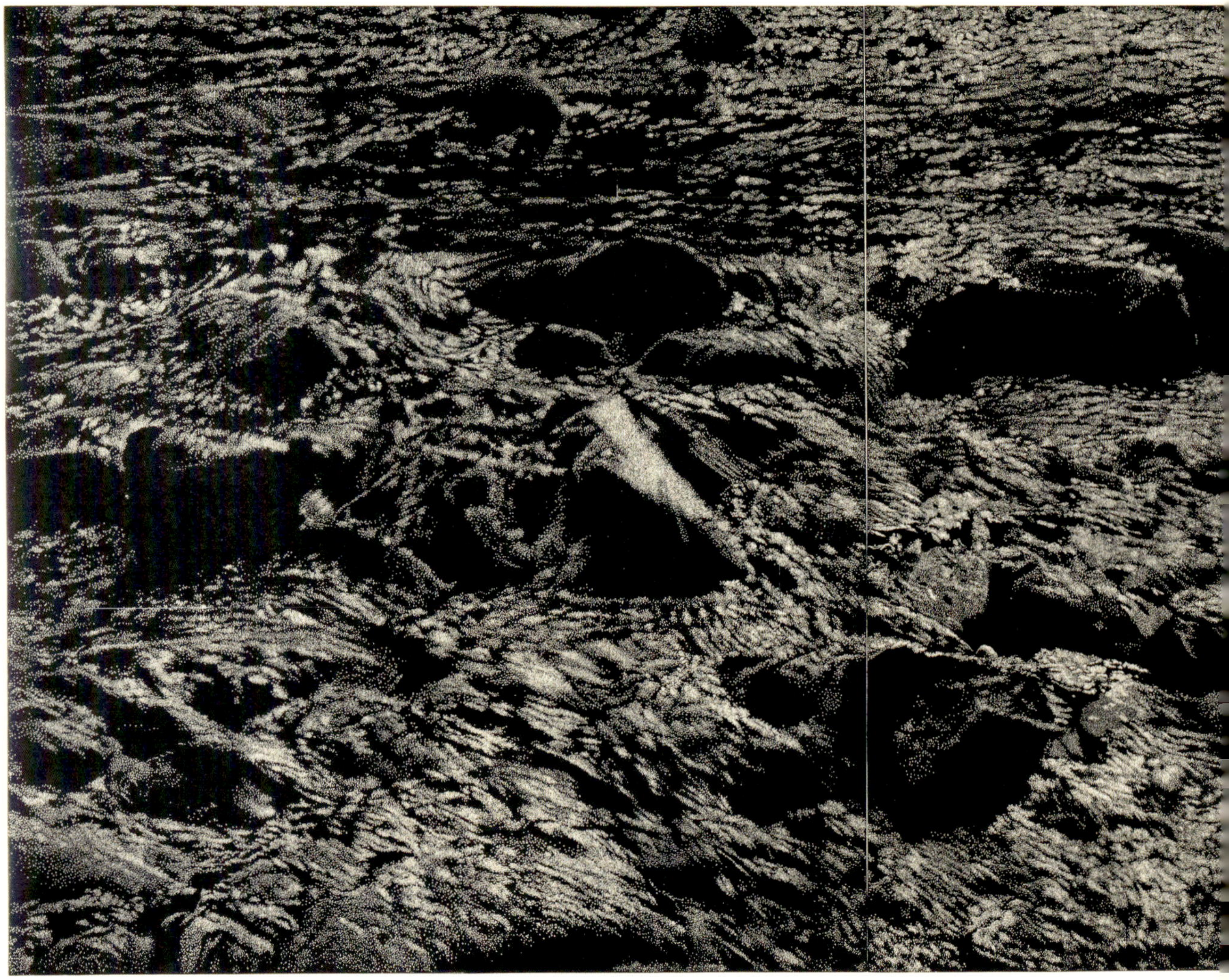

Schwarzwasser II, 1994. Woodcut (3 plates), 202 x 183 cm each
Hand-pulled print on hand-made Kinkaku Japan paper, 212 x 627 cm. Black
Private collection, Cologne

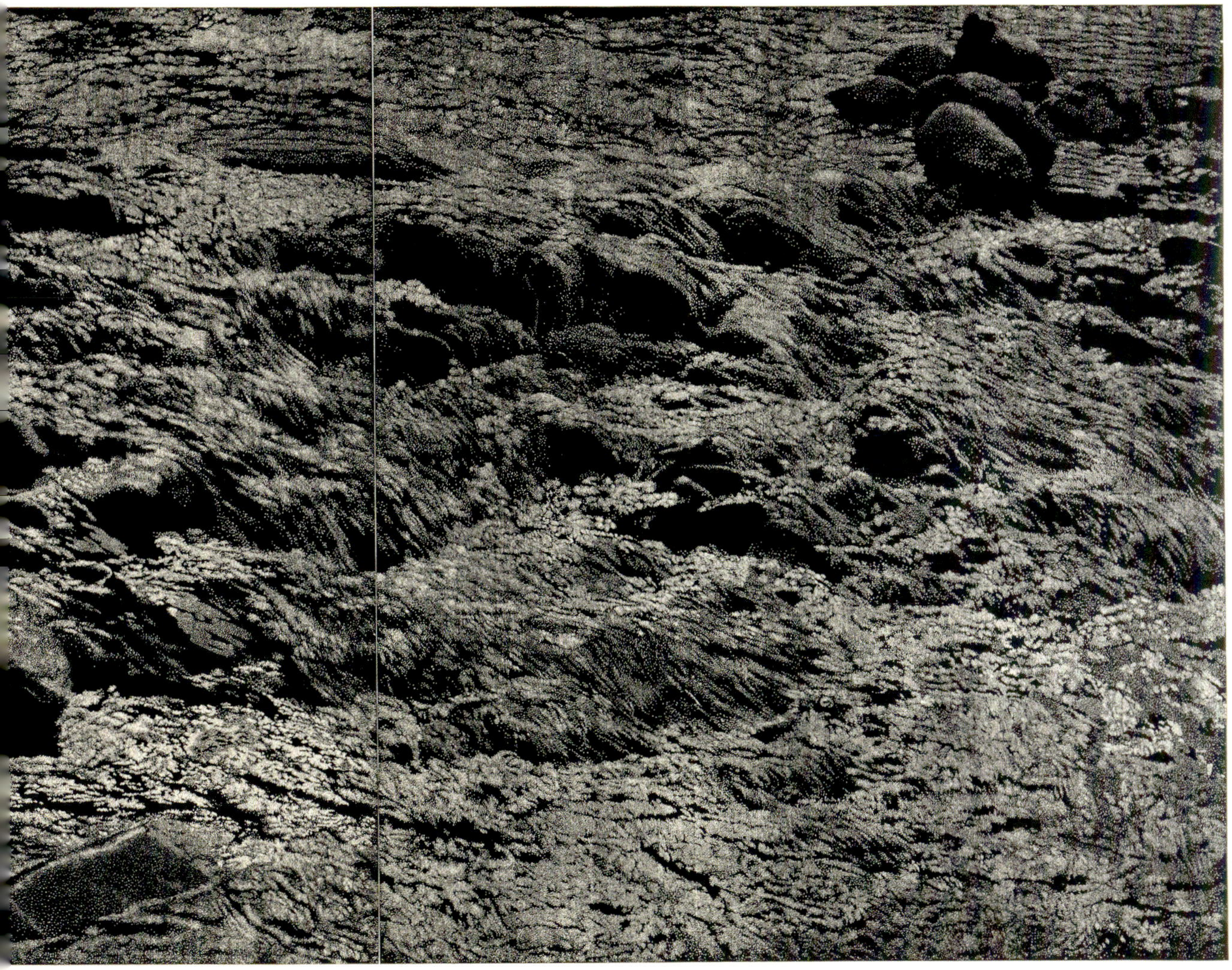

AUTUMN

Franz Gertsch's *Retrospective* had arrived in Vienna in late 2006. On a Sunday morning, the artist and I visited the Brueghel Room in the Kunsthistorisches Museum. Immersed in thought, Gertsch stood before Brueghel's *Return of the Herd* (autumn), the *Hunters in the Snow* (winter) and *Gloomy Day* (early spring), going back and forth between the three canvasses. What these paintings, known to him for a long time, had in common – the horizon, the rural Flemish setting, the characteristic story – fascinated him. It was here that Gertsch – who had also always stopped time in his pictures, and also devoted himself to variations on a theme – experienced the final impulse for a cycle of seasons, which had existed as an idea for quite some time already. How presumptuous at his age to tackle such a colossal project, which would certainly claim five years of his life! This was a feeling shared by Gertsch himself, who turned eighty while working on his Four Seasons cycle. He was plagued by doubts as to whether he would complete the series throughout the entire process. After a ten-year break in painting, he had produced only seven canvasses since 1995: *Gräser (Grass) I–IV*, and *Silvia I–III.*

Gertsch decided on a landscape theme from the immediate surroundings of his home in Rüschegg in the canton of Bern, which had provided him with so many subjects. He also opted for a monumental picture, whose size would be more than three metres high and almost five metres wide. The theme of the new cycle was a stretch of woods on a slope on his property, with a small footpath – leading to the village church – along which he walked every day. He plunges into this visually impenetrable wild underbrush and explores it pictorially from A to Z in four giant-format paintings. The thicket is complex, but not at all primeval in nature – no romantic majesty, just a random, nondescript place.

Underbrush and thicket that catch the eye, impede the view of the distance and put themselves centre-stage initially became worthy of illustration, albeit in the small format of the *paysage intime*, with the Barbizon school.

In the portrait of autumn the colours are muted, the trees in the foreground already bare, the ground already tinged brownish with fallen leaves. Only with effort does the eye find its way through this brown-green landscape, composed of these two colours as well as their countless shades between black and white. On the right half of the painting, camouflaged by the light, the young, thin tree trunks, which could also be the branches of a bush, strive upwards. Their partly overlapping stable lines form vertical elements in a network composed of branches, as fantastic as it is comprehensible as a spatial web. The left-hand side of the painting, however, is more enclosed. Dark-green leaves, now and then flashing dazzling white from a dappling of sun, frame the centre that opens out into the depths of the picture, revealing a more open spot: a small clearing covered in reddish-brown-golden leaves. The eye's trajectory over this picture resembles a maze-like path; when focusing on the thicket, all details of the moment are pictorially described – clarified, as it were – with the greatest precision. At the same time, we repeatedly become entangled in the spatial structure. Only after long, intensive contemplation – a highly focussed observation – do we 'understand' this scenic place, recognising, for example, a fragment of sky shimmering through the leaves, which helps in positioning the dimensions.

Autumn is the first painting in the four-part 'Seasons' series. The choice of subject turns the landscape into a frame-filling theme. There is no way out. At the same time, *Autumn* is a reflection on painting. The two-dimensionality of this medium, emphasised here by the 'all-over' covering of branches and leaves, is just as present as the subject of dissolution.

With paintbrush and mind-boggling palette, the loss of the saturated green and the dissolution of the unit 'tree' into leaves and branches are recreated. With its nuanced colour-scheme and its tracing of space, *Autumn* represents a splendid starting-point to Franz Gertsch's 'Four Seasons' series.

Guido de Werd

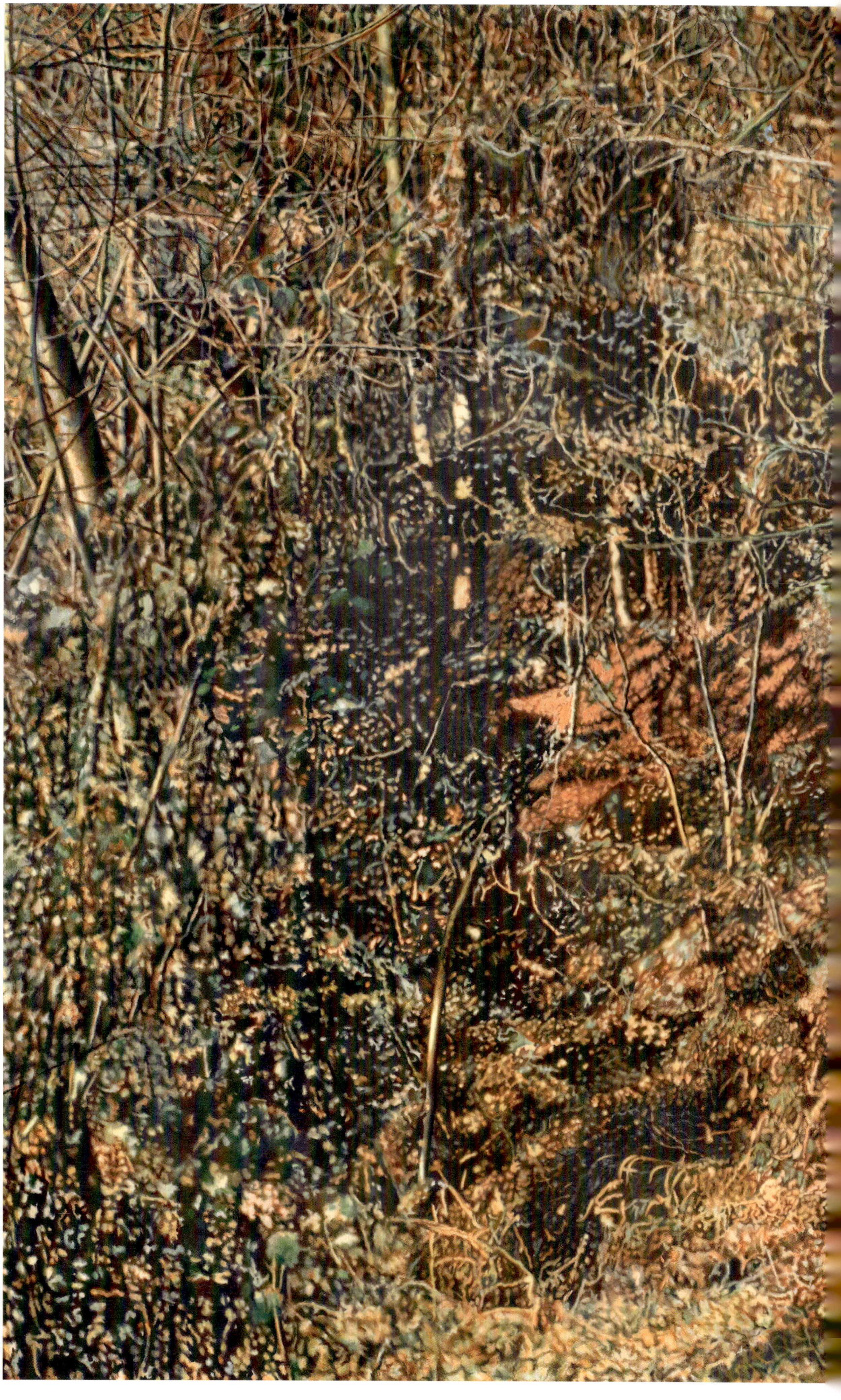

Autumn, 2008
Acrylic on unprimed cotton
canvas, 325 x 490 cm
Collection of the artist

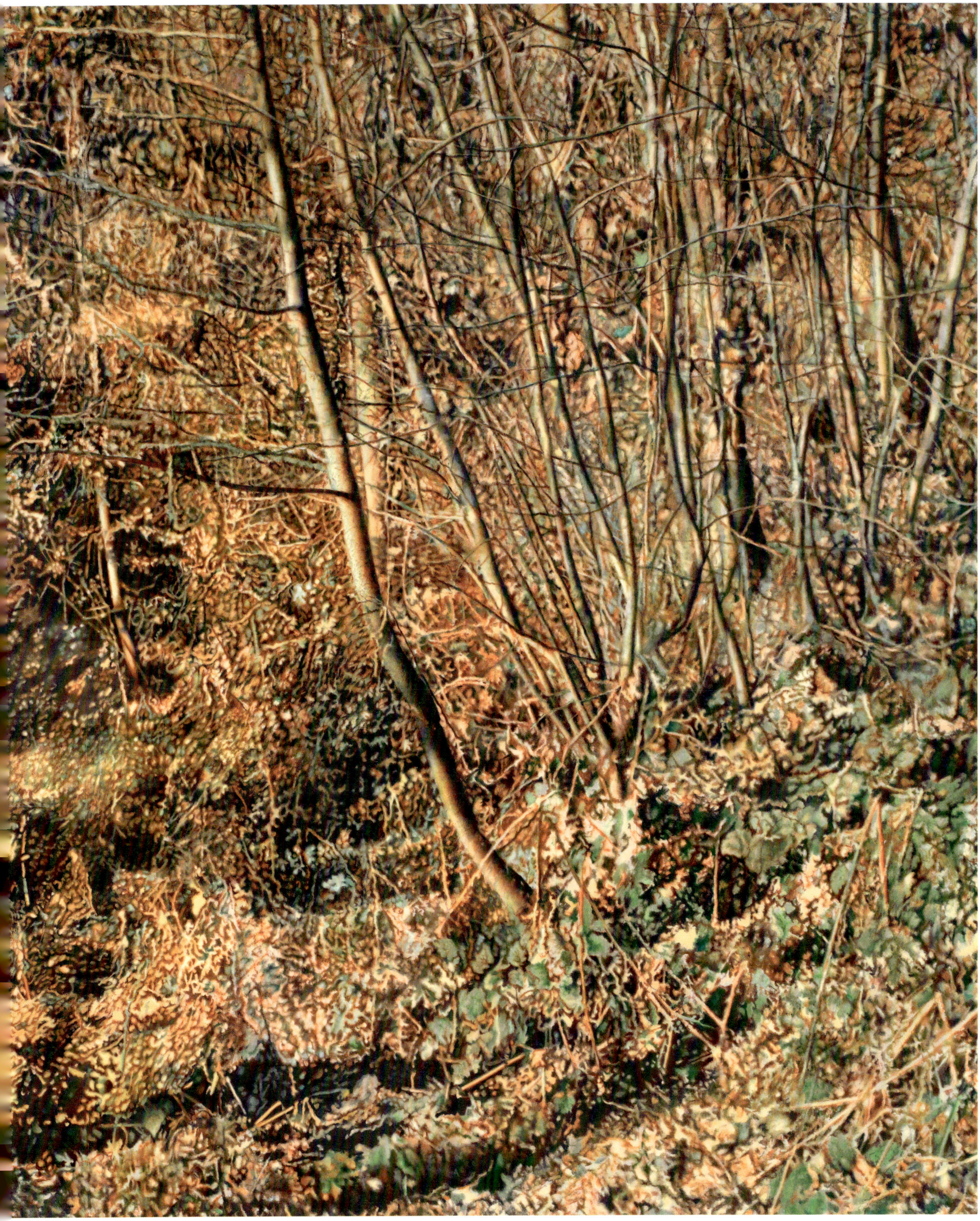

Johanna I, 1984
Acrylic on unprimed cotton
canvas, 330 x 340 cm
Private Collection

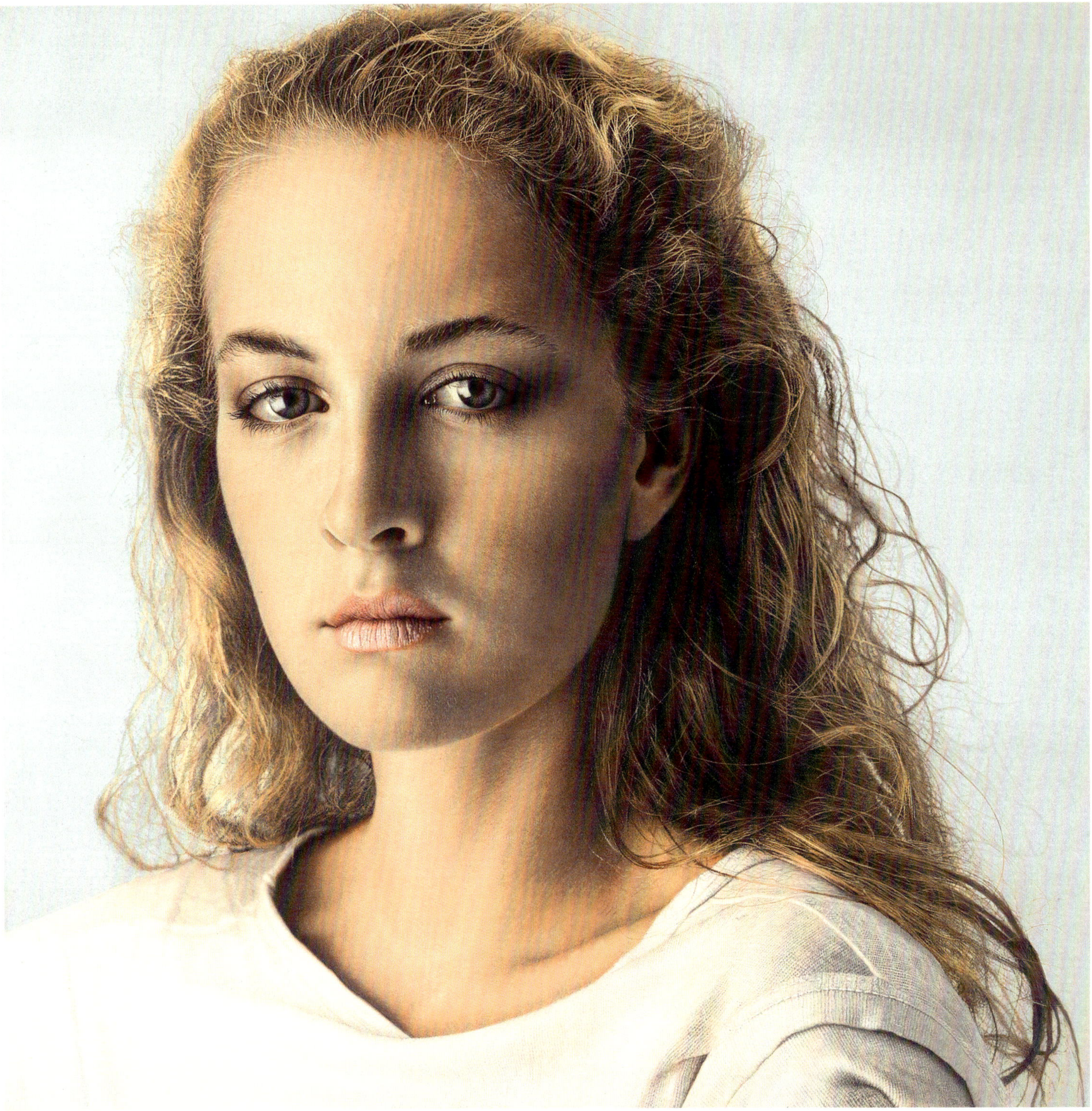

Natascha IV, 1988
Woodcut (1 plate), 232.5 x 182 cm
Hand-pulled print on Kumohadamashi Japan
paper made by Heizaburo Ivano, 276 x 217 cm
Yellow, 1/18. Collection of the artist

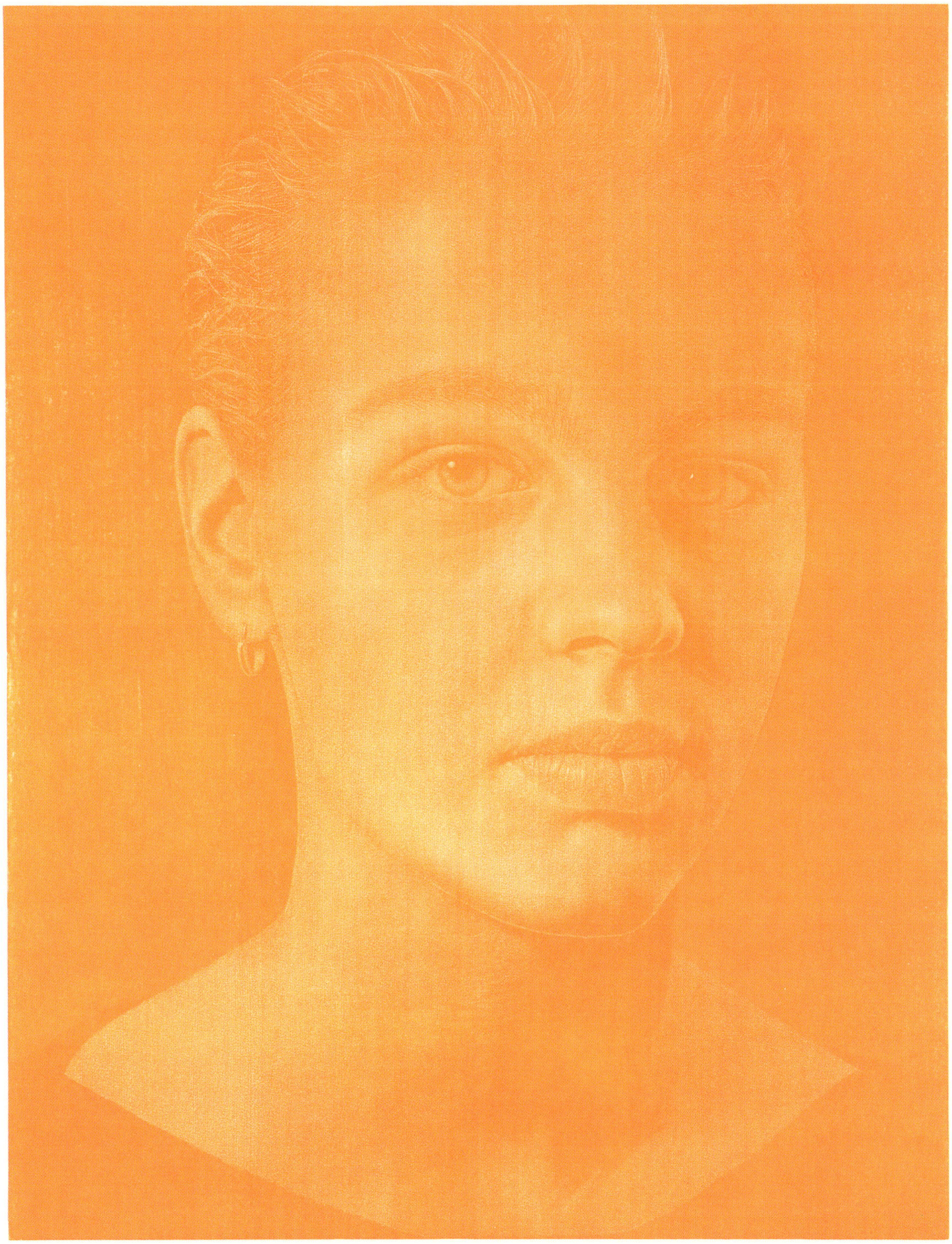

Natascha IV, 1988
Woodcut (1 plate), 232.5 x 182 cm
Hand-pulled print on Kumohadamashi Japan
paper made by Heizaburo Ivano, 276 x 217 cm
Red (deep), ea. Collection of the artist

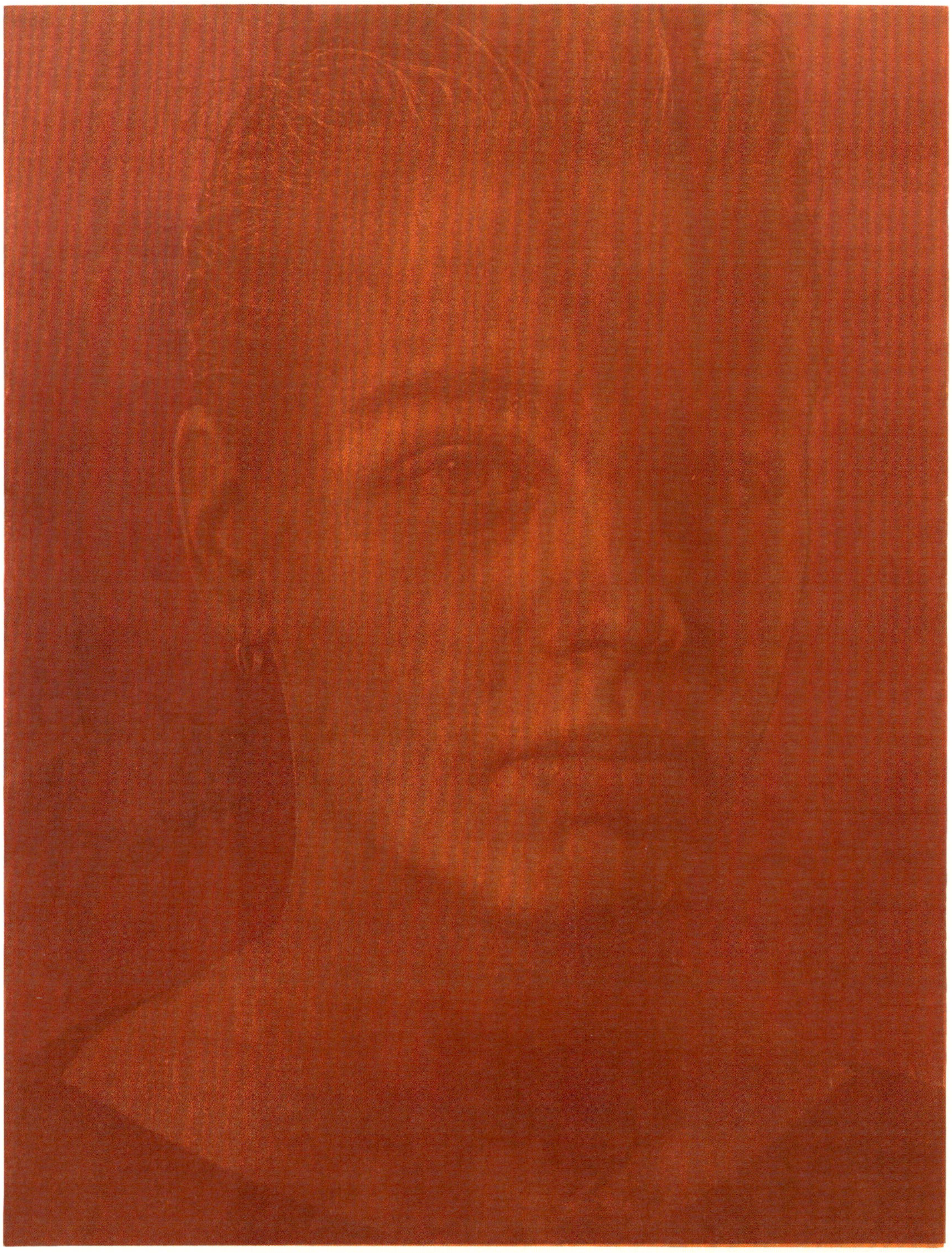

Natascha IV, 1988
Woodcut (1 plate), 232.5 x 182 cm
Hand-pulled print on Kumohadamashi Japan paper
made by Heizaburo Ivano, 276 x 217 cm. Green, 8/18
Property of the Swiss Confederation, Federal Office
of Culture, Bern (deposited on permanent loan at the
Kunsthaus Zürich)

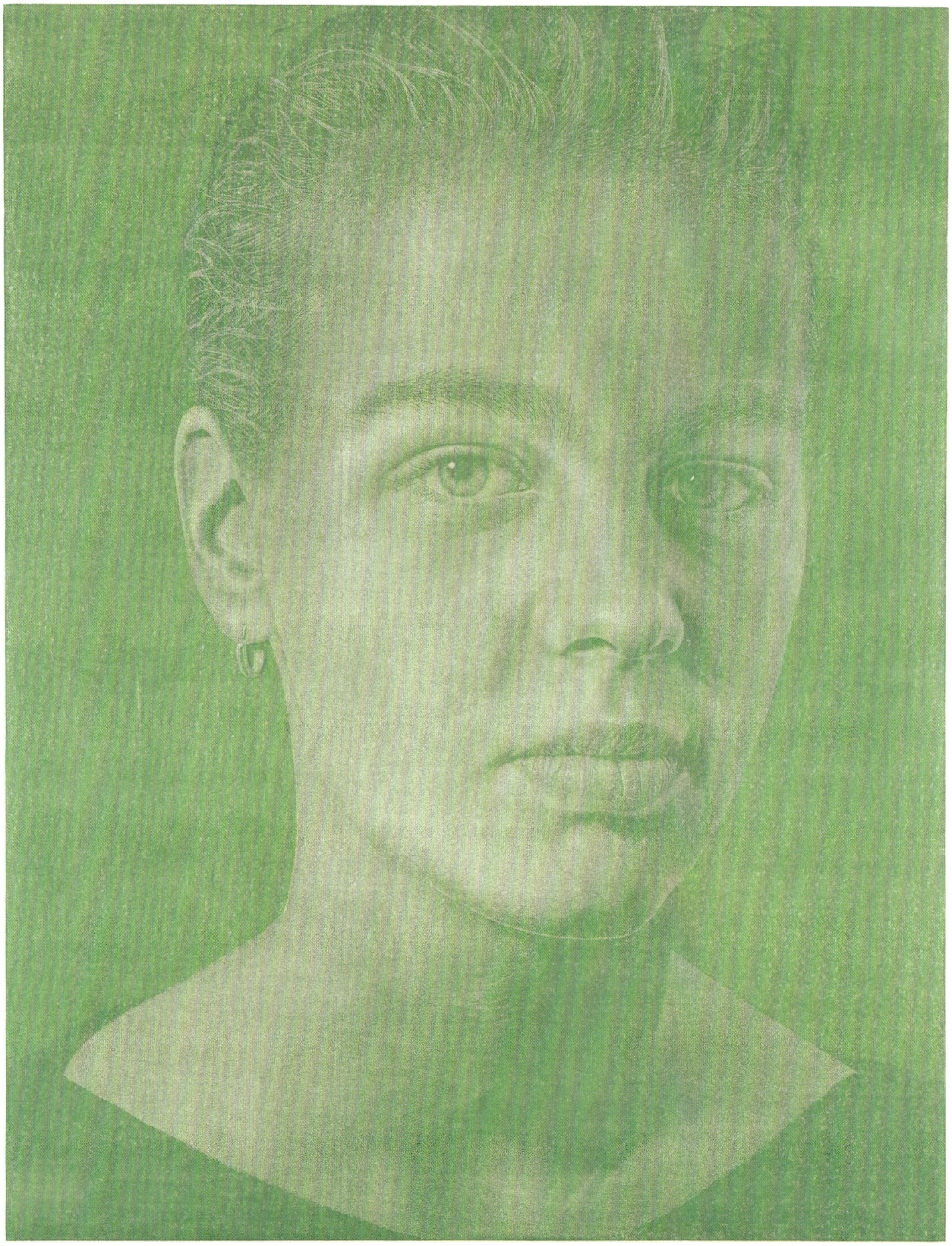

Natascha IV, 1988
Woodcut (1 plate), 232.5 x 182 cm
Hand-pulled print on Kumohadamashi Japan paper
made by Heizaburo Ivano, 276 x 217 cm
Mid-blue, 14/18. Collection of the artist

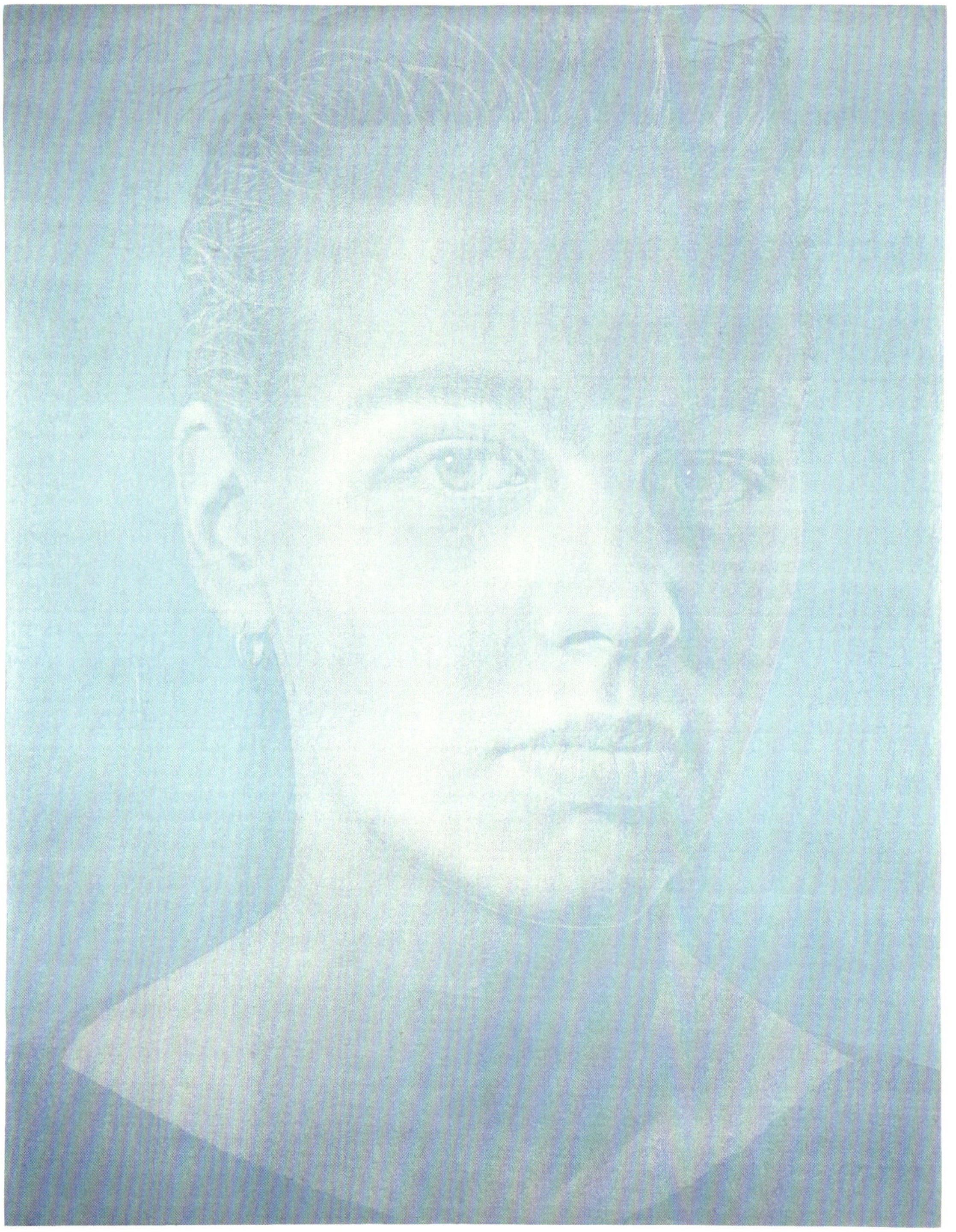

WINTER

The virtuosic naturalism and giant format of Franz Gertsch's winter landscape suggest that we are looking at none other than a late magnum opus of photorealism. The artist's method of working also seems to bear this out, given that the projection of a slide onto the canvas preceded the creation of the image. To this extent, the painting always becomes the reproduction of a reproduction. Added to this is the unpretentious detail extracted from a concrete piece of nature in the immediate vicinity of the artist's residence and studio. If we also consider the conscious elimination of a personal signature, we definitely appear to be dealing with a late work of photorealism, albeit one which has replaced Gertsch's earlier portrayals of the 1970s lifestyle with the unruffled serenity and slower pace of old age.

But *Winter* belongs to a four-part cycle based on the theme of the four seasons, and therefore it already provides a foretaste of the symbolism of natural growth and decay, which is part and parcel of the genre. Taken in its totality, the cycle can be read as a philosophical commentary on the 'life of nature' as well as the 'nature of life'. *Summer* deals with the impenetrability and abundance of life in all its vividness. Conversely, with its colouristic invasion of the snow, the *Winter* canvas tells of the cold occupying the land, and of that stillness in which everything freezes rigid.

This painting does not portray an event. It is a picture of a state: there are no ice-skaters, no returning hunters. Snow is lying, not falling. For Franz Gertsch, the snow yields an infinite abundance of light cushions and heavy blankets, burying everything beneath them like a shroud: snow and cold as the great levellers, when warmth has escaped from the body.

In *Summer*, under the brushwood, behind the foliage or in the dark shadows of the woods, one can sense hidden life: creatures searching for a safe haven. A crackling and rustling come from the impenetrable thicket. Although the fall motif is more transparent, the shape of the autumn-tinged woodscape prevents the glance from penetrating the depths of the undergrowth. The warm, reddish-brown streaks of colour conceal more than they reveal. After all, given the nature of the season it illustrates, new life is inherent in *Spring*. It is an amiable painting, easy and pleasant to step into and then to walk along the path and cross over the little wooden footbridge, dipping into the depths of the forest. Above all, *Spring* offers an enormous spatial experience. By contrast, *Winter* represents a thermo-physical event, without the space losing depth.

In *Winter*, everything is visible, from the outermost foreground and its dry undergrowth to the sparse, lignite-black trunks towering far into the forest. These woods are silently sleeping their long, death-like winter sleep.

Viewers who would rashly identify an example of landscape painting as an expression of subjective perception in this late magnum opus are off the mark. Gertsch is no romantic, no matter how melancholic and gloomy the painting of the snow may be.

The landscape detail portrayed in his 'Four Seasons' cycle actually exists. It is a genuine piece of nature. The woods with their path are not the product of the artist's imagination; they are no *capriccio*. And yet this deciduous forest could be found anywhere; it cannot be pinned down to a specific place.

To experience the effect of the four paintings, it is essential to encounter the originals and drawings, if only for their sheer size. What was true for the dramatically motivated nature of the heroic landscape for entirely different reasons – for reasons of subject – also applies to Gertsch's 'Seasons' cycle: each of his paintings overwhelms the viewer. But not because of their formal pathos or their heroic objects; in other words, not because of bizarre cloud formations, dramatic lighting effects, towering mountain ranges or stormy seascapes. Gertsch's 'Seasons' overwhelm in the same way as Jackson Pollock's similarly monumental Drippings: because, like the latter with their all-over structure and seemingly borderless picture margin – and viewed from the proper distance of a few steps back – they are larger and wider than the viewer's field of vision.

Franz Gertsch's 'Seasons' wed the small landscape detail, known to us from the close-up of the *paysage intime*, with the monumental, realistic landscape panoramas of the Barbizon school. By their very nature, pictures of this size cannot be painted *en plein air*; rather, it is only because of their naturalistic aesthetics and design principles that they can pretend to be open-air paintings. They take shape not in front of their subject but in the studio where, for an entire year, Gertsch worked with great discipline on each of the four seasons. Gertsch alters the photos that serve as models only minimally, in details. The true achievement of execution lies in the pictorial unity of these enormous canvases. Gertsch massages not just every detail into the rough canvas; nature itself seems to have been massaged into the painting. Image and nature, the reproduction of the projection, have become one.

Equipped with the credibility of an objective inventory, and provided with the sacraments of the symbolism already inherent in any seasonal cycle, Gertsch's four monumental paintings tell of nature's perennial cycle of death and renewal.

Klaus Albrecht Schröder

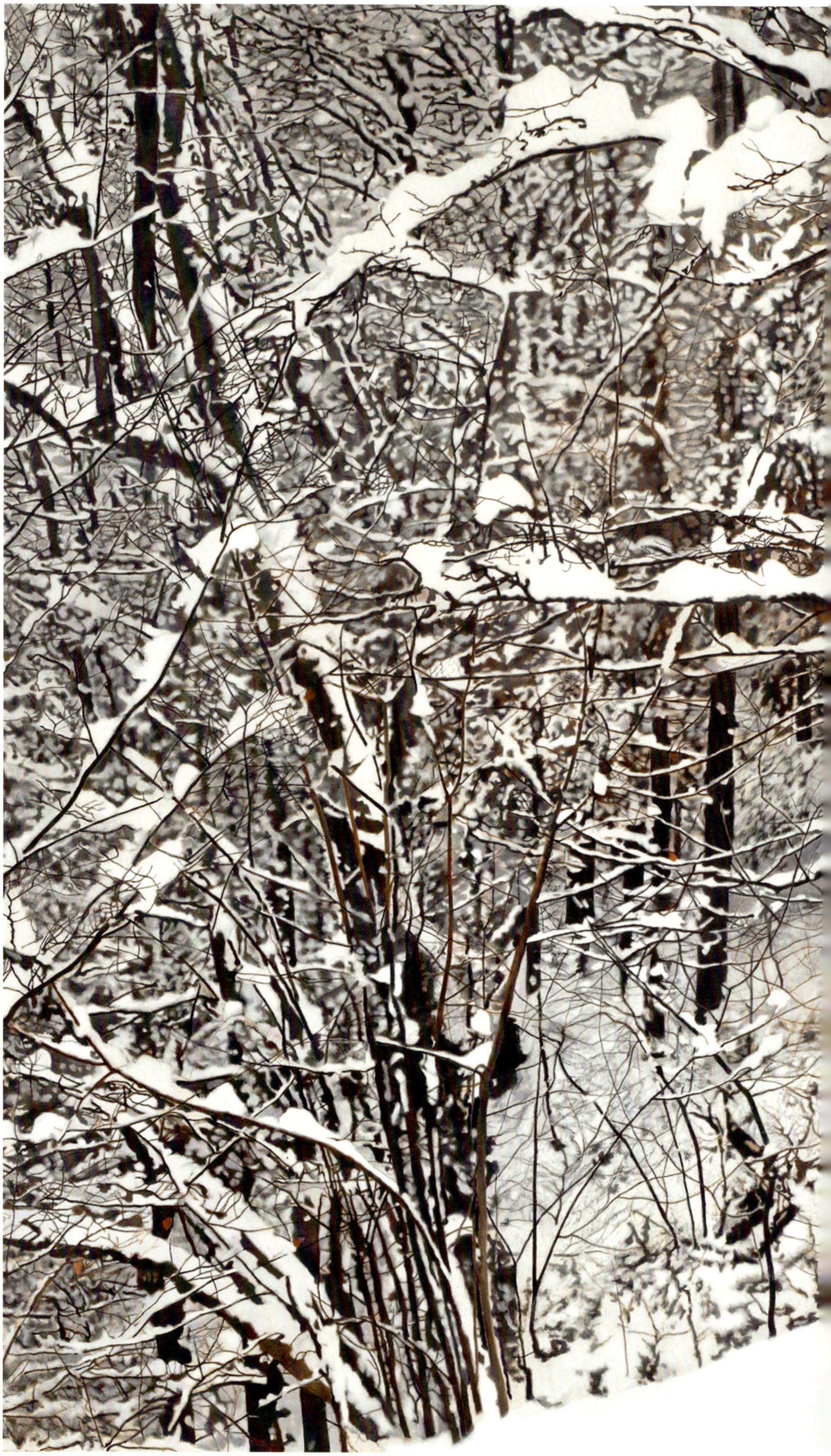

Winter, 2009
Acrylic on unprimed
canvas, 325 x 480 cm
Collection of the artist

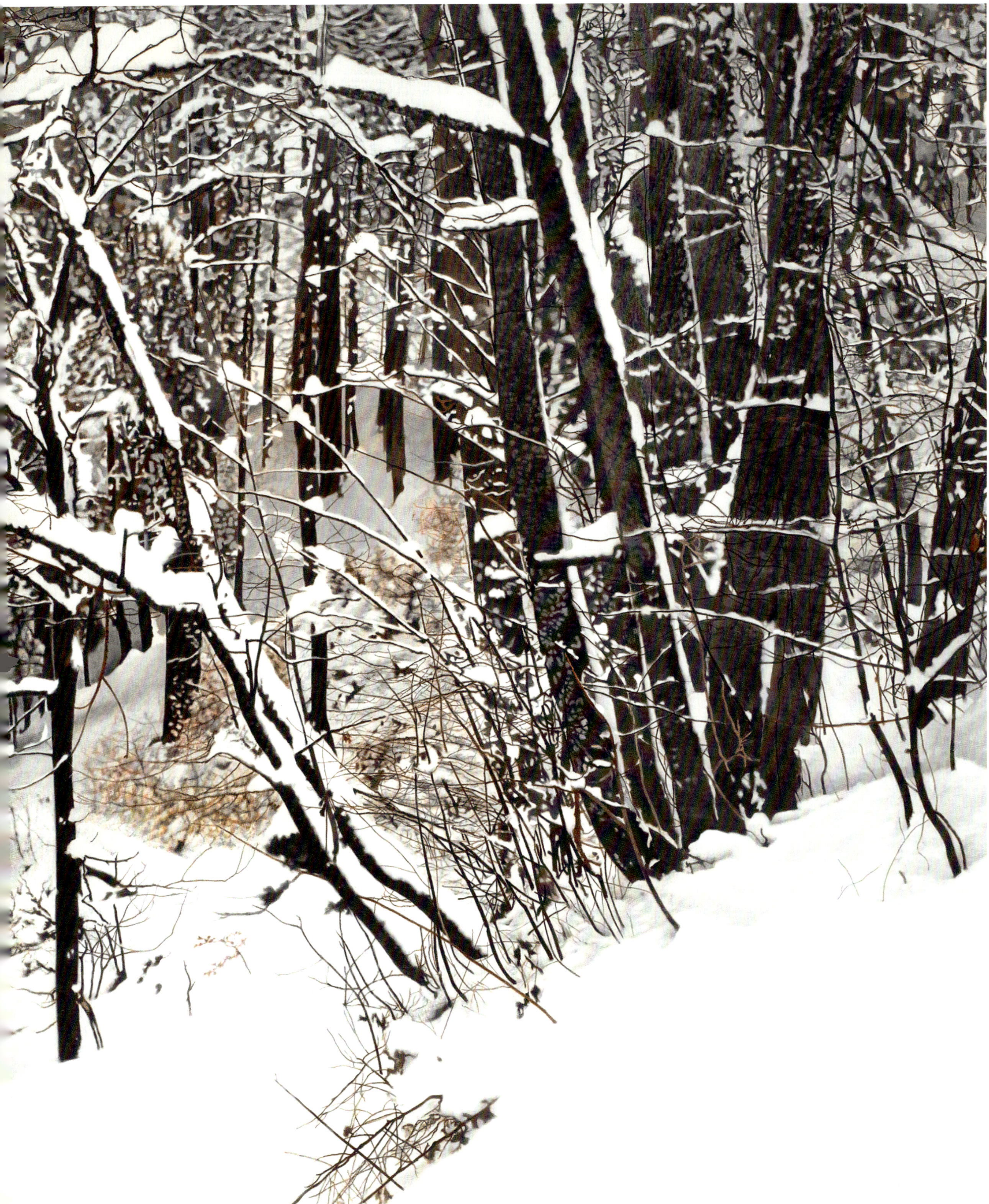

Silvia III, 2004
Mixed technique (egg tempera and resin-oil paint)
on unprimed cotton canvas, 315 x 290 cm
Collection of the artist

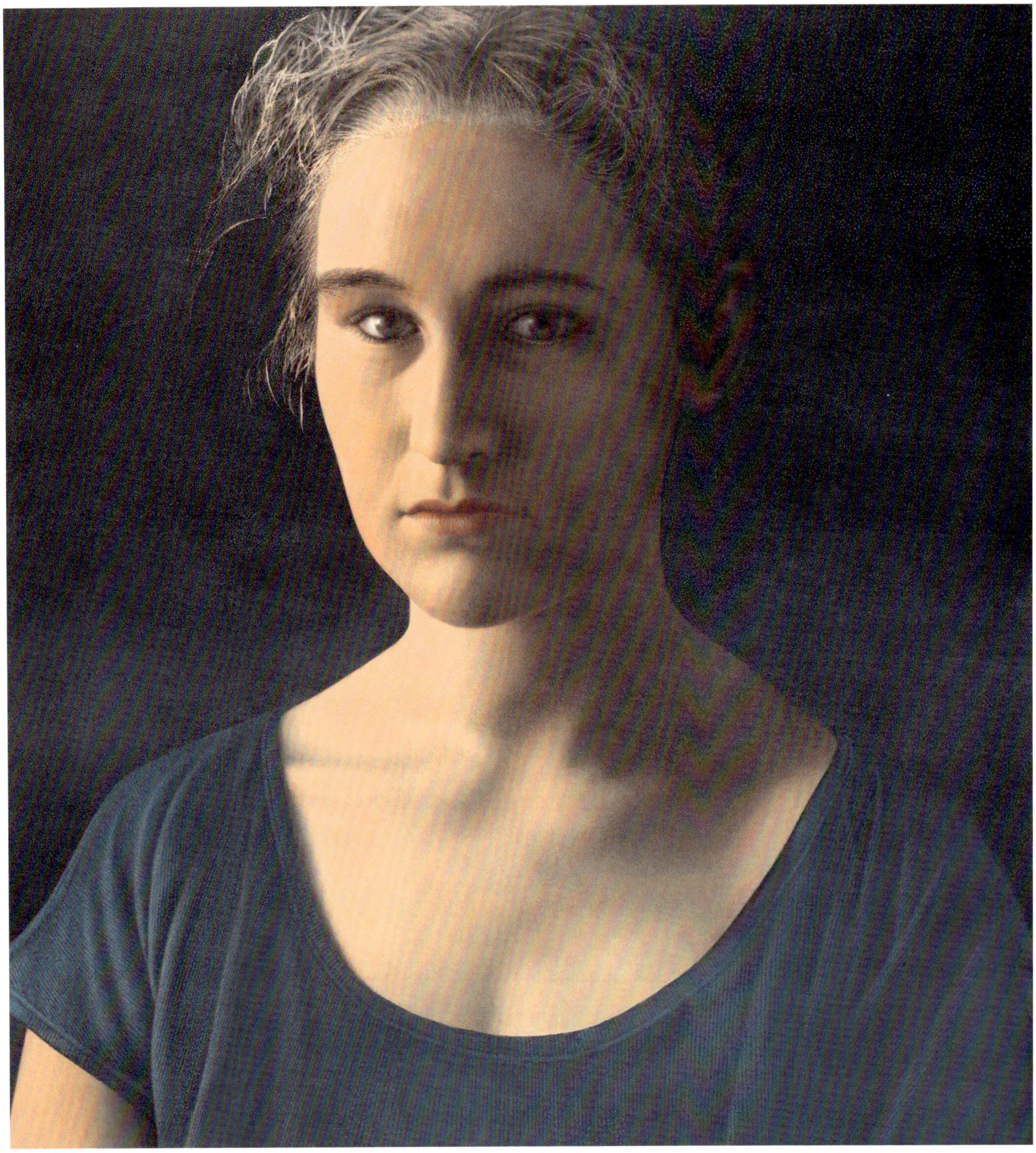

Diptychon Schwarzwasser, 1995
Woodcut (2 plates), 212 x 157.5 cm each
Hand-pulled print no. 6 on Kumohadamashi Japan
paper made by Heizaburo Ivano, 276 x 380 cm
Watery blue. Collection of the artist

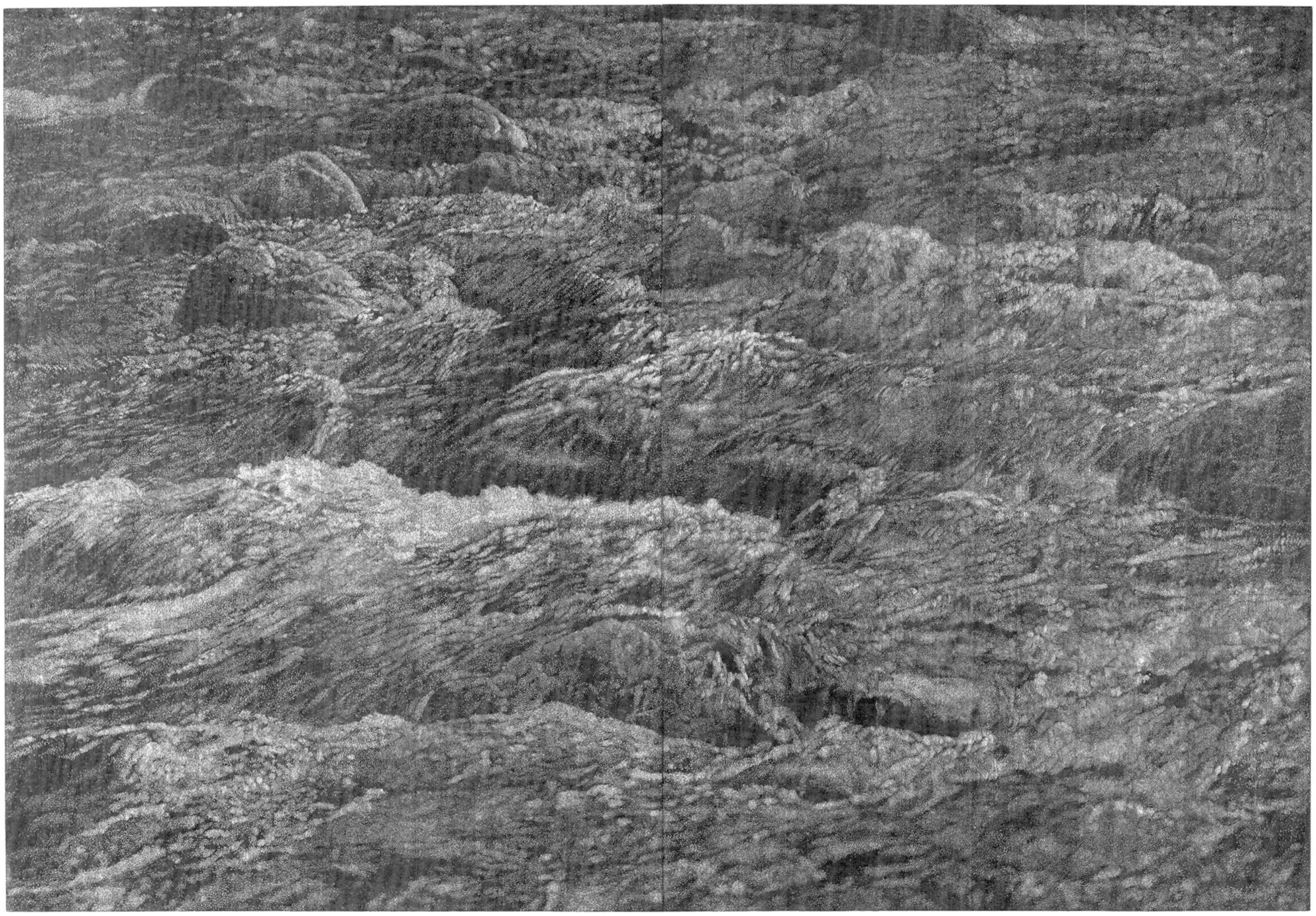

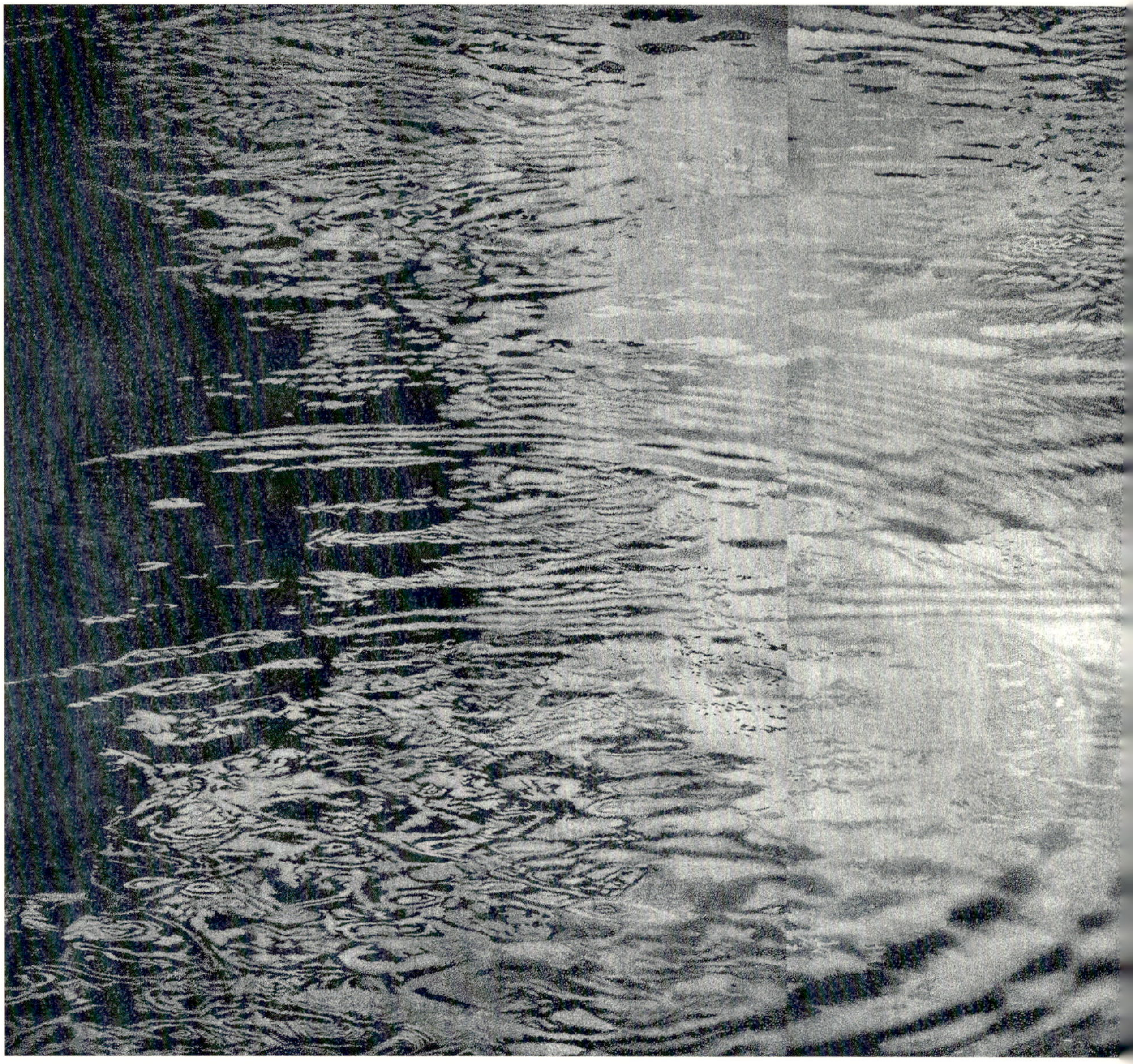

Triptychon Schwarzwasser, 1991/92. Woodcut (3 plates), 237 x 185 cm each. Hand-pulled print no. 6 on Kumohadamashi Japan paper made by Heizaburo Ivano, 276 x 217 cm each, 276 x 597 cm in total. Midnight blue. museum franz gertsch, Burgdorf

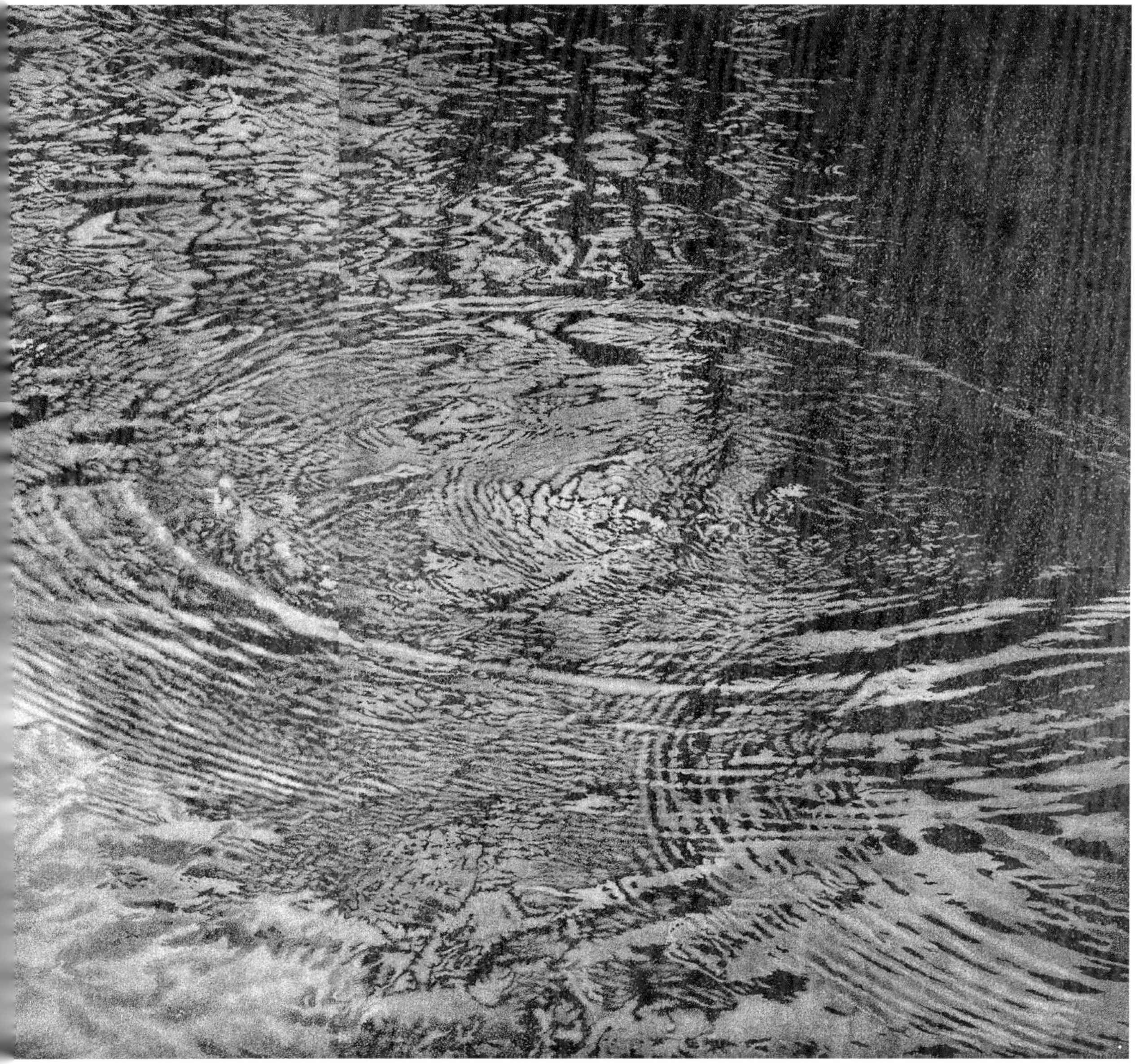

Doris, 1989
Woodcut (1 plate), 218 x 157 cm
Hand-pulled print on Kumohadamashi Japan
paper made by Heizaburo Ivano, 276 x 217 cm
Light grey, ea. Collection of the artist

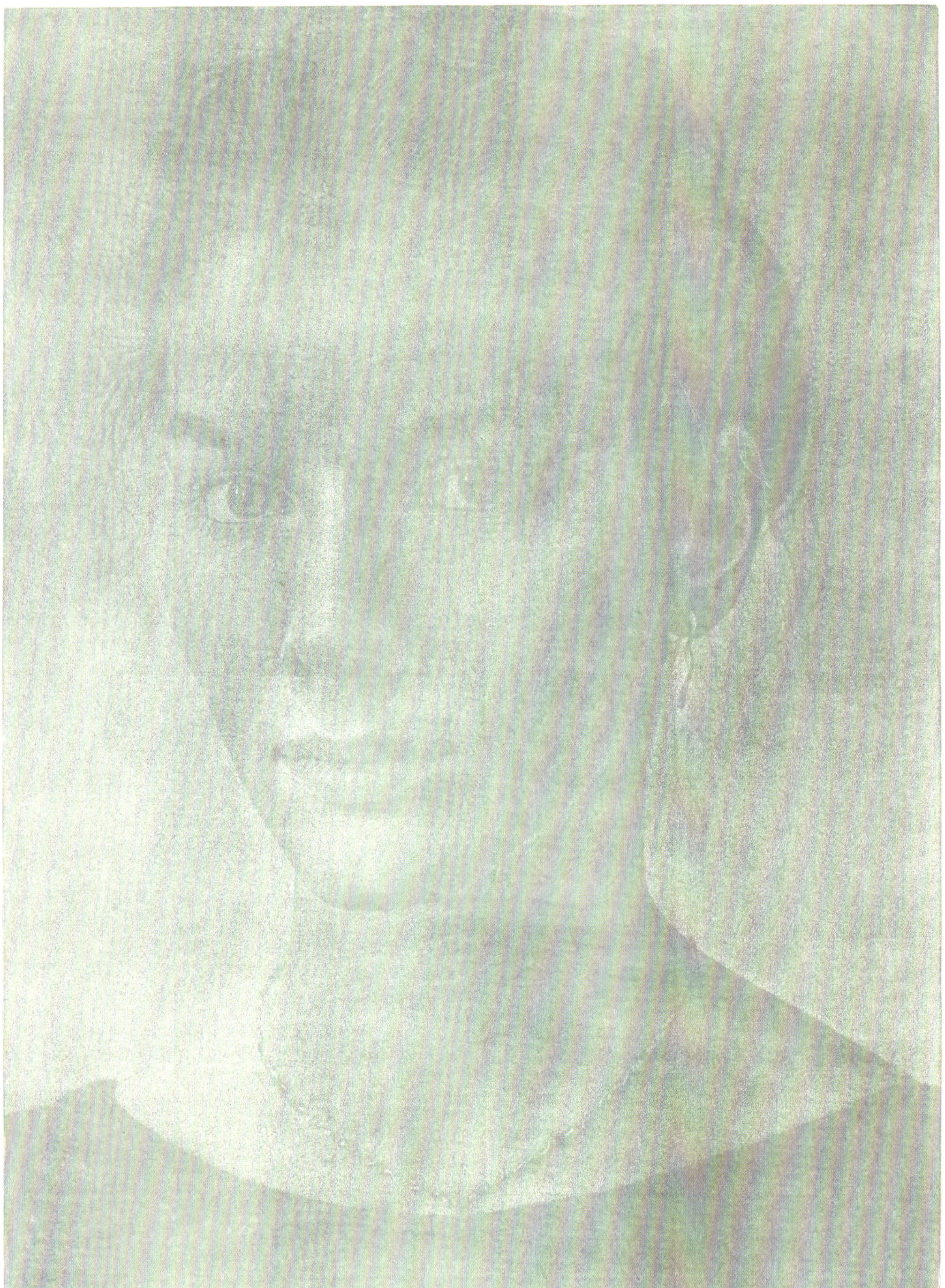

SPRING

> *'Occasionally, something that was hidden in the light becomes visible in the shadow.'*[1]

All four of Franz Gertsch's seasons paintings are based roughly on the same viewpoint. 'Roughly' means that, according to the artist, the photographs on which the paintings are based were all taken within a radius of about seven square metres. The path into the heart of the woods depicted in the photos remains clearly recognisable only in *Winter* and *Spring*; in the cases of *Autumn* and *Summer*, this is literally obscured by the paintings.

Spring measures 325 x 480 centimetres. The picture is painted on an unprimed cotton canvas. While the other three works have been done in acrylic, here Gertsch has used egg tempera. Egg tempera consists of three components: egg yolk, equal parts of linseed oil and damar varnish, and water. According to the artist, the advantage of this medium is that it can create softer transitions, as well as allowing the paint to be rewetted on the cotton canvas over the course of a working day. By contrast, acrylic binds instantly and is difficult to rework. The difference between the two media is scarcely visible in the final effect, but the extreme density of the painting in question meant that egg tempera was the preferable option.

Franz Gertsch laboured on the picture for sixteen months in total, painting for up to 5 hours a day and sometimes covering a surface of no more than 20 x 25 centimetres. Although a 4 x 6 centimetre transparency served to pinpoint the picture's various parts and their structure, Gertsch never painted in the light of the slide projector – instead, the picture took shape under artificial lighting conditions (daylight tubes). The reason for this is, to a certain extent, self-explanatory: natural daylight would have been too uneven.

Rather than beginning painting at the top left and stopping at the bottom right of the picture, Gertsch started to the left of the path. Next came the expansion, in what might almost be described as concentric circles, with each area seamlessly opening up a new area.

What does spring look like at 900 metres above sea level? The photograph was taken in the early morning on a day in late April. The quality of the light clearly suggests the very beginning of spring, and has a peculiar wanness that the artist himself at times refers to as almost depressive. The early spring is awaiting an infusion of warmth. In just a few days, there could be an explosion of colour. Not here and now, though: the leaves are tiny. Flattened by snow, autumn foliage is still visible on the path; the light blue of the sky is far away in the distance; no 'scents of spring' are yet perceptible – but everywhere is the greening of new growth.

So much for the first, most general, level of observation. The second arises when we look closely at the picture's structure. As in the *Winter* painting, the viewer's gaze is drawn almost automatically to the path leading into the heart of the woods. This path cuts diagonally into the pictorial space, makes a noticeable turn to the left, follows over a footbridge, and then disappears in the depths of the forest. Grouped around the path are trees, some with almost excessively long branches. One can also see the shadow of beech trees. The concept of choreography is evoked, and the term is justified to the extent that, in some cases, Gertsch has intensified the tonality of the echelons of vertical, diagonal and roughly horizontal tree elements ranging into the depths, as they have too little substance in the slide itself. Once one has apprehended this choreographic feat, it is branded on the memory for good. Even more important, though, is the following occurrence: that suddenly, amidst the generally sallow appearance of the painting, a wealth of colour emerges. At times these colours possess the transparency of a watercolour, forming a pattern woven in gentle gradations, flickering like light in the delicate yet dense branches of the trees. Whole worlds are discovered in this detail of a world, begging the question as to which is the part and which the whole.

Placing a light passe-partout, with a window measuring 29 x 25 centimetres, over sections of the painting, I marvelled at how one 'picture' after another revealed itself. The autonomous density of the parts is breathtaking. Once again, though, one can say that their sum does not yield the whole. This is true when, taking a leaf out of Emmanuel Levinas' book, we consider the puzzling transcendence[2] of the whole. If, however, we start from the energetic viewpoint of field theory, then every phenomenon within a field size is treated similarly and according to standardised perspectives, with the aim of capturing the whole and the parts in a qualitative equivalence. The 'coordinate transformations' considered to be significant would then be found at the point where sharpness and fuzziness meet, where depth becomes surface and surface becomes depth, where the structure is crucial for the picture, and where it diverts attention from itself: where space-filling light becomes 'palpable' through individual light sources.

The time factor also plays a decisive role in these paintings of Gertsch's. The daily achievement of a 20 x 25 centimetre area creates a compression whose effect is comparable to that of a gravitational force. It is essential to cancel this out by transferring the autonomy of the parts into the coherence of a light-filled sounding-box.

Five hours' painting a day, over a period of sixteen months, presupposes the painter's faith in the characteristic style of the painting – a painting that downright demands this thoroughly specific style. The painting, or photography, invites a range of possible interpretations, but the 'system' is inexorable. It is the artist's task to transcend this. Time becomes permanent: a concentrated trancelike state, focusing emotional, mental and painterly energy. Standing in front of the painting, one imagines the painting willing the act of its creation to remain secret, almost as if it had painted itself. Rather than appearing as a brilliant individual achievement, the act of creation is revealed as a 'coming into being', as a continuity in time and space, connected with that 'mysteriousness' to which Levinas refers. And we ask: Why does someone do something that apparently runs counter to the basic principle of creativity? Artists must harvest their world, stubbornly and patiently. They must be 'original' in the sense of 'genuine' or 'first of their kind', rather than in the sense of 'innovative'. Anyone contemplating Franz Gertsch's œuvre will be amazed at the way that, even in his youth, his realistic and tender force soaked up the figurative with a downright obsessive energy – and this at a time after the Second World War, when abstract and *informel* ('formless') art were in the spotlight. For many, the Lucerne exhibition of 1972, especially the cult painting *Medici*, marked the artistic birth of the then-42-year-old. Yet to think so is a mistake. Although so-called photorealism was a transatlantic theme – the *Medici* painting was consequently also shown at *documenta 5* in 1972 – its roots go back much further than this, and the continuity is genuine. The Seasons paintings, and particularly *Spring* as the last and perhaps most demanding of the series, show us how Gertsch conceptualises his painting. He knows how to change it, adapting it to each new theme.

Franz Gertsch definitely doesn't practise a style. He doesn't turn painting up over a theme like a cuff on a shirt sleeve. Instead, an osmosis occurs between the model and the canvas. There is a devotion in evidence that consists of infusing the models with life – as if, through the permanence of the commitment, it were their wish to experience the transformation as an act of creation, or to make it capable of being experienced as such. As if the models were like the shadows in Plato's cave allegory, which yearn for the knowledge of reality.

The 'four seasons' paintings express the fundamental curiosity of the artist Franz Gertsch, and his desire to explore the world: an 'eternal recurrence', but never the same way twice! Or, in the words of Jacques Derrida: 'Equality of difference and of repetition in the eternal recurrence.'[3]

Jean-Christophe Ammann

1 Hiromi Kawakami, *Am Meer ist es wärmer ['It's warmer by the sea']*, Munich 2010, p. 185.
2 See Katharina Bahlmann, *Können Kunstwerke ein Antlitz haben? ['Can works of art have a countenance?']*, Vienna 2008, p. 24.
3 Quoted in: Janina Wellmann, *Die Form des Werdens – Eine Kulturgeschichte der Embryologie, 1760–1830 ['The form of becoming – a cultural history of embryology, 1760–1830']*, Göttingen 2010, p. 29.

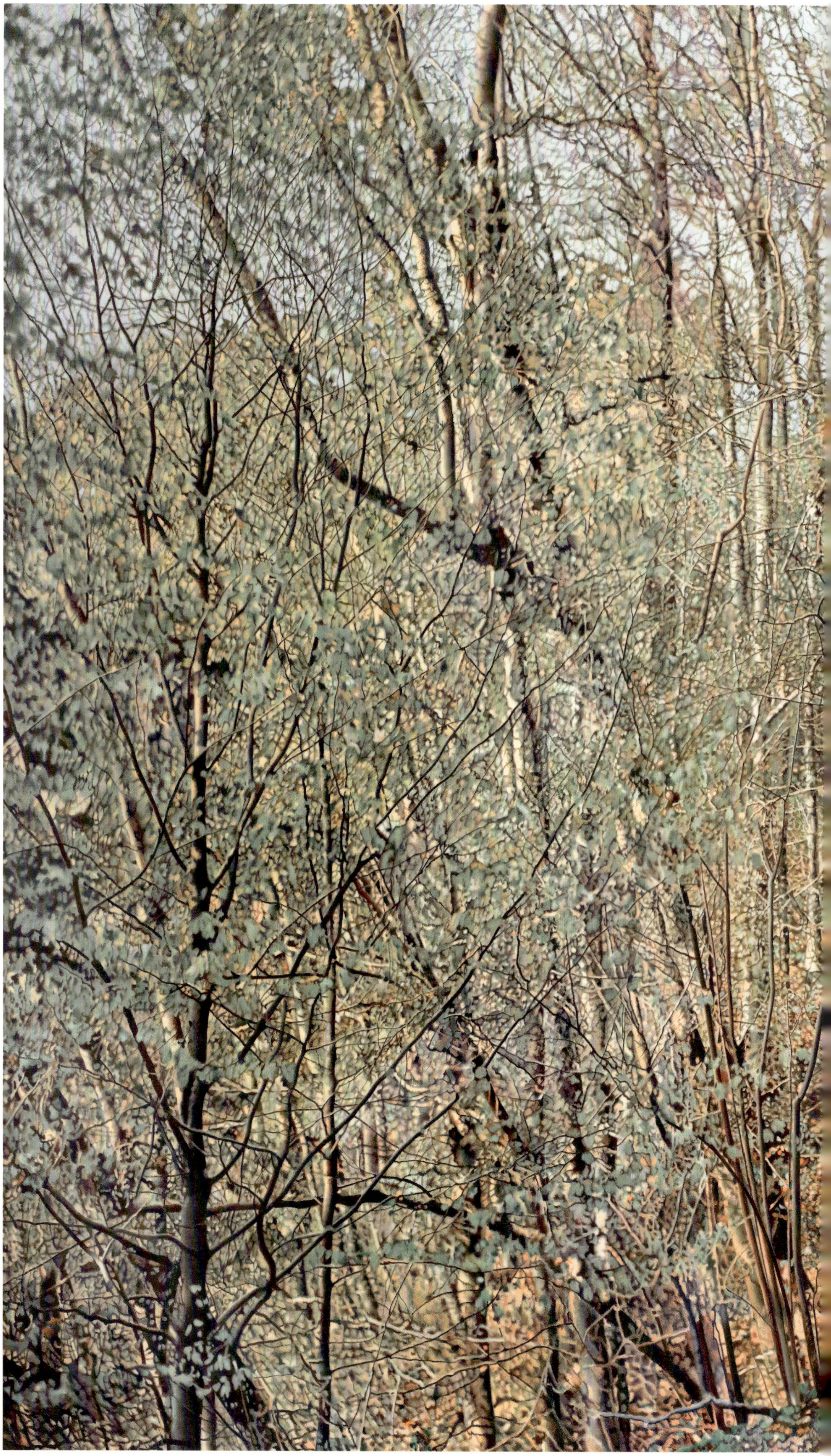

Spring, 2011
Egg tempera on unprimed
cotton canvas, 325 x 480 cm
Collection of the artist

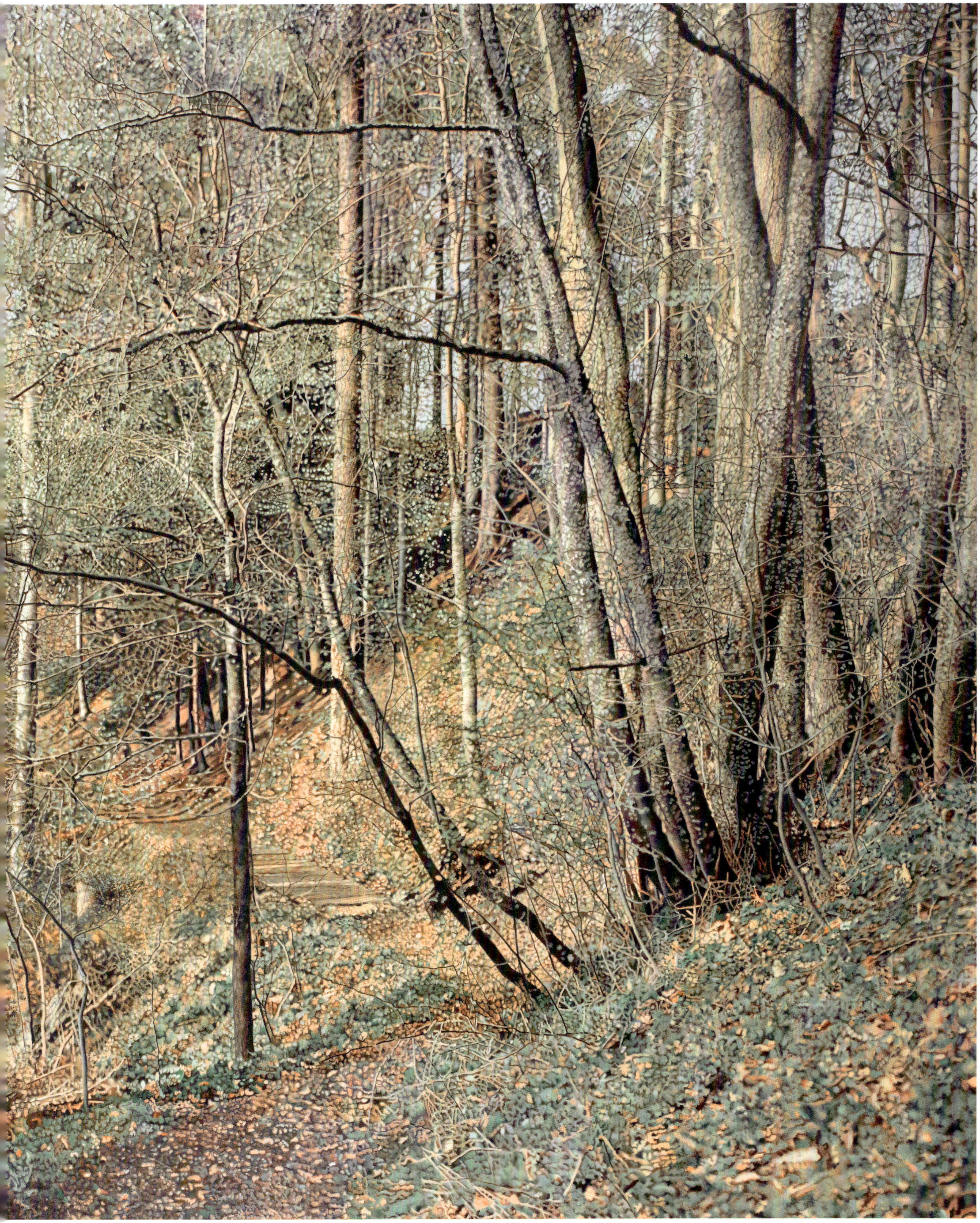

Silvia II, 2000
Egg tempera on unprimed
cotton canvas, 300 x 290 cm
Museum Kurhaus Kleve, Freundeskreis
Museum Kurhaus and Koekkoek-Haus
Kleve e. V.

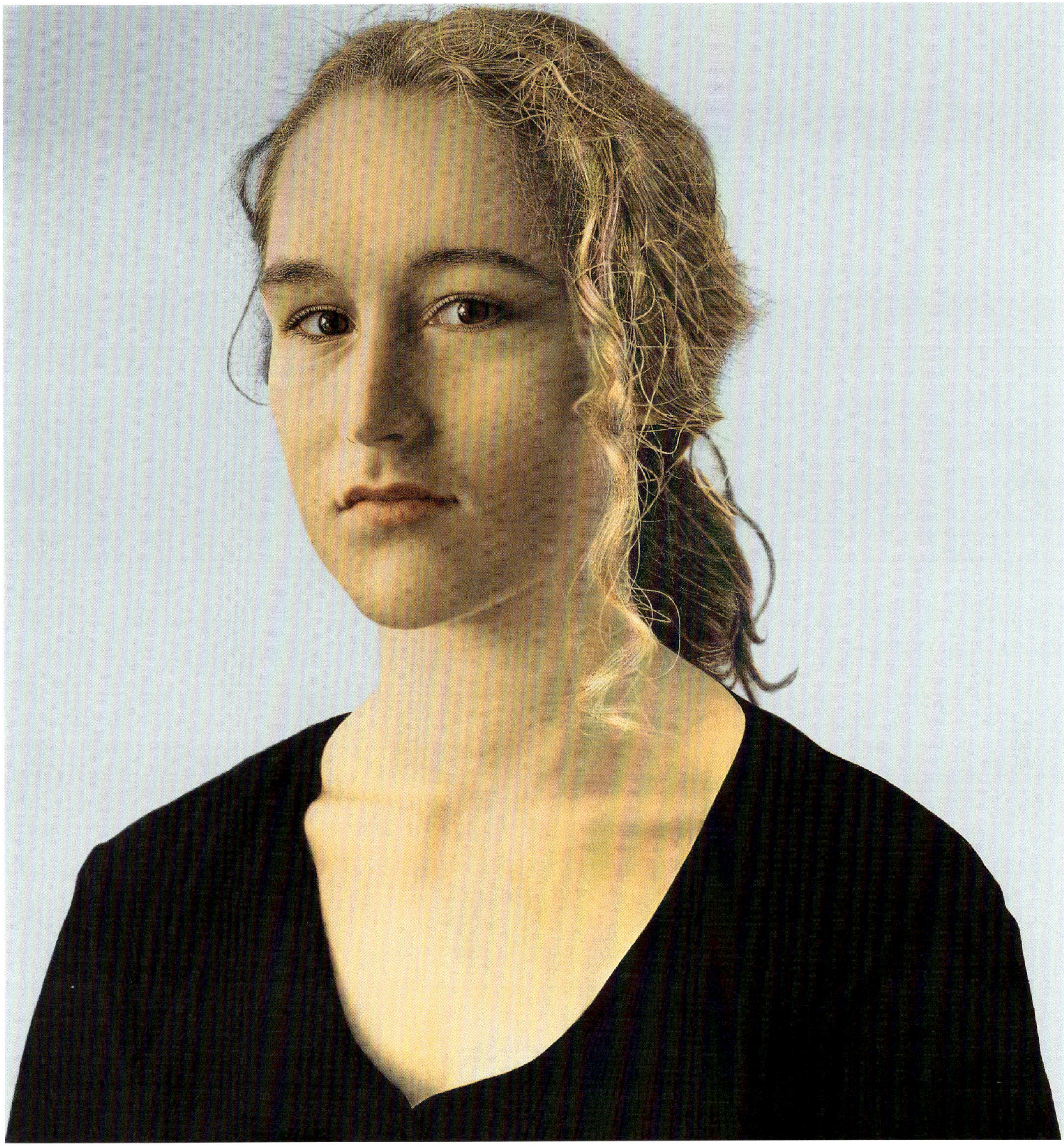

Dominique, 1988
Woodcut (1 plate), 234 x 181 cm
Hand-pulled print on Kumohadamashi Japan
paper made by Heizaburo Ivano, 276 x 217 cm
Blue-grey (lapis lazuli ash), 17/18
Collection of the artist

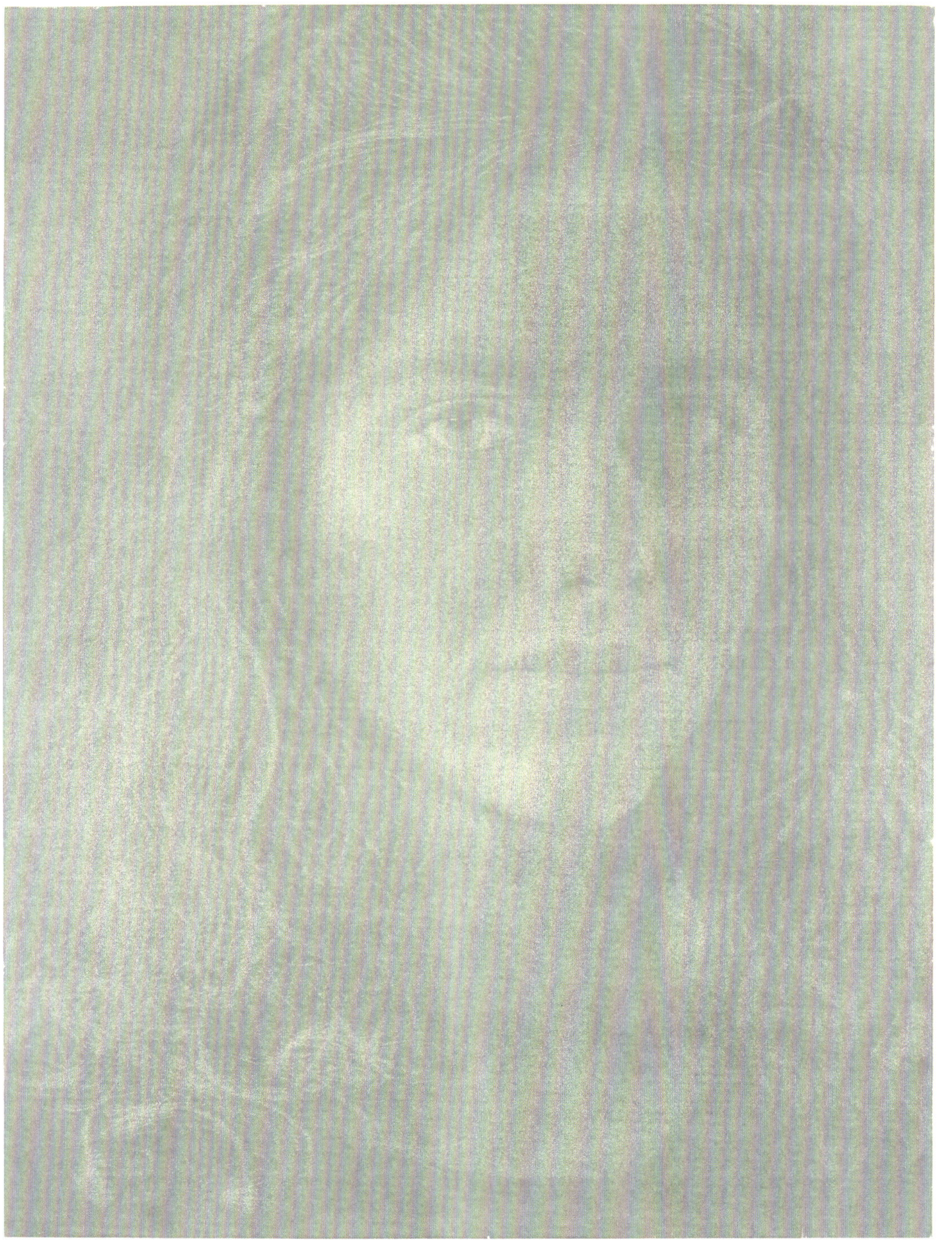

Dominique, 1988
Woodcut (1 plate), 234 x 181 cm
Hand-pulled print on Kumohadamashi Japan
paper made by Heizaburo Ivano, 276 x 217 cm
Malachite, 2/18
Collection of the artist

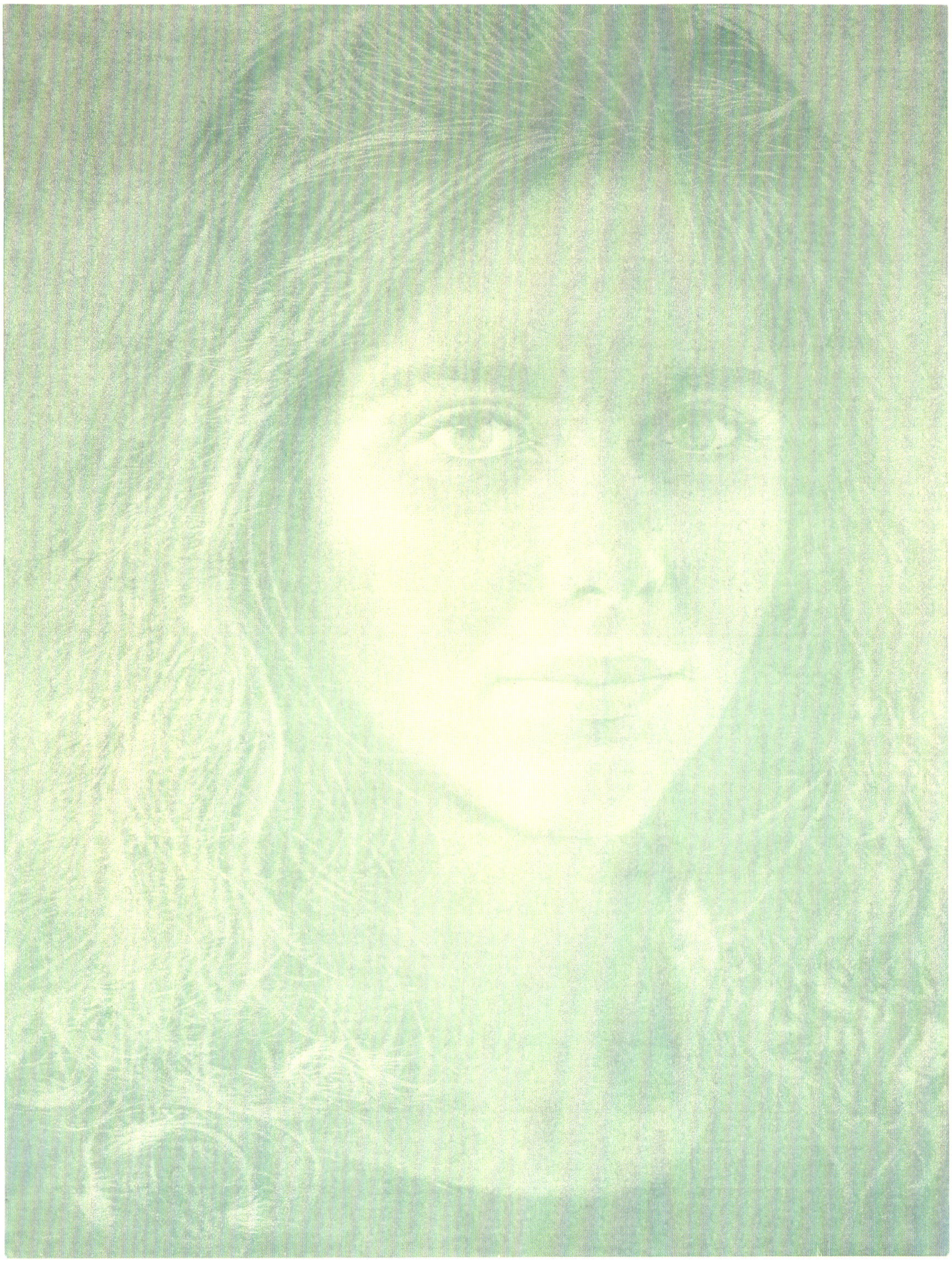

Dominique, 1988
Woodcut (1 plate), 234 x 181 cm
Hand-pulled print on Kumohadamashi Japan
paper made by Heizaburo Ivano, 276 x 217 cm
Honey-coloured, ea 6/7
Collection of the artist

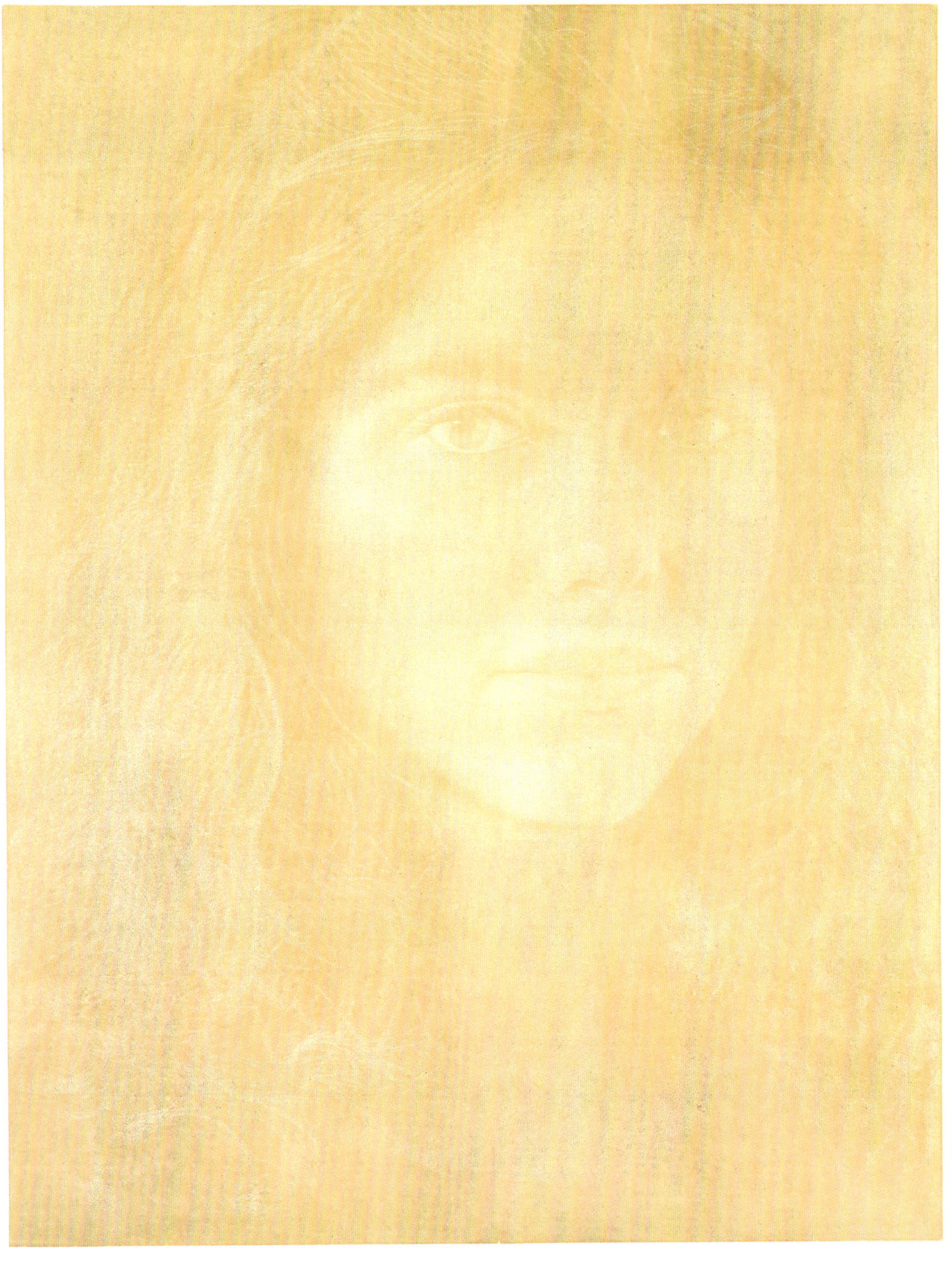

Dominique, 1988
Woodcut (1 plate), 234 x 181 cm
Hand-pulled print on Kumohadamashi Japan paper
made by Heizaburo Ivano, 276 x 217 cm. Purple, 1/18
Dr. h.c. Willy Michel Collection

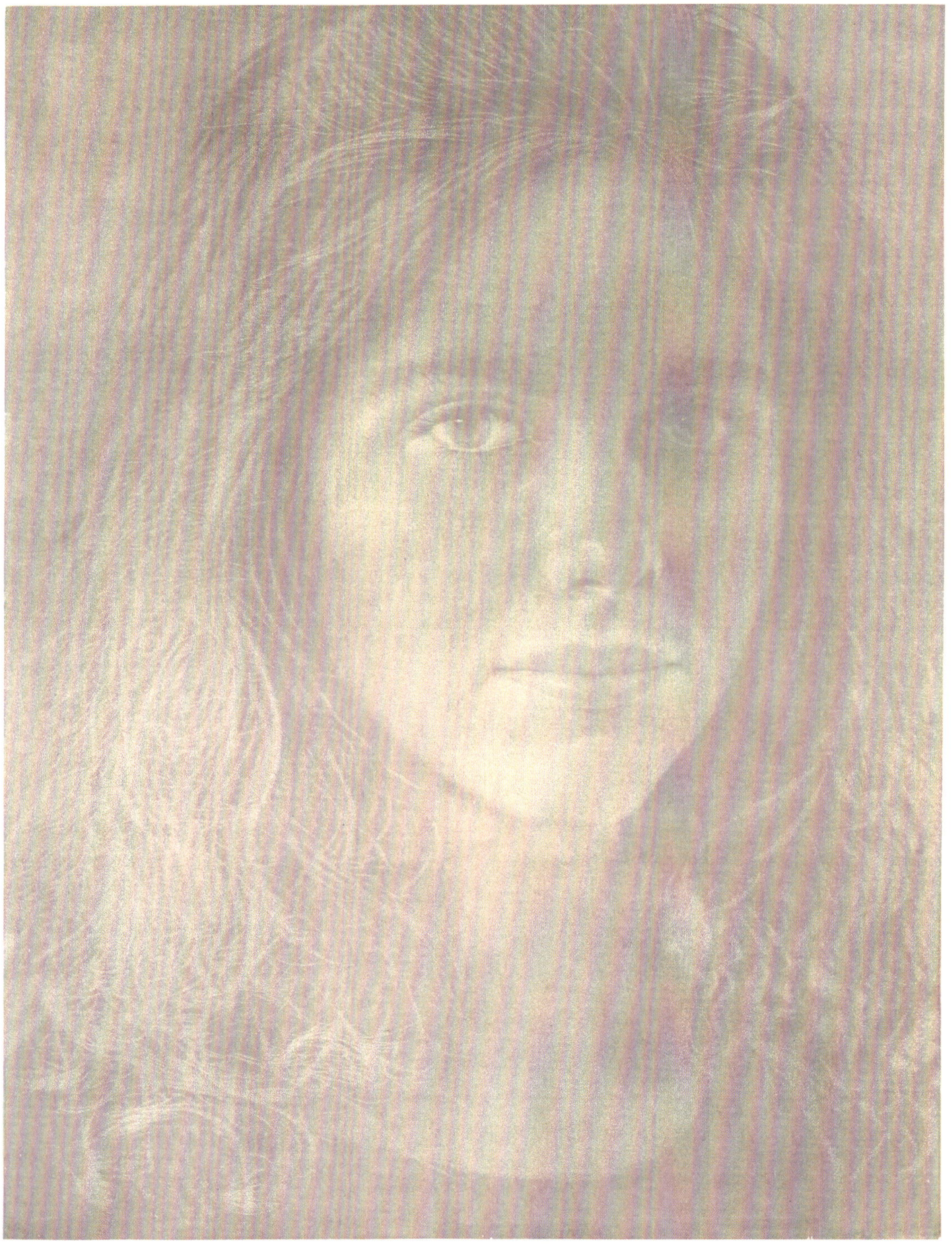

SUMMER

Thicket of Life (Summery)

Were a viewer able to move about with all his senses in this tremendously compressed painting, he or she would see myriad points of light, a flickering and glimmering between foliage and branches, a flashing of trunks and leaves, darkness in the shadowy depths. He or she would smell the scent of the earth and grass, feel the still midday heat, and breathe the spicy forest air. The complexity of the synaesthetic sensations which Franz Gertsch's work *Summer* is capable of triggering can only be sketched briefly here; even so, its holistic effect before the original is palpable in every detail. For it is not just the stupendous variety of the visible that proclaims this opulent detail of the world as a veritable apotheosis of the earthly; above all it is the intensity and imaginative power, with which all summery modes of being ever experienced, remembered or dreamt have been conjured up and compressed into a substantial 'personification image'. This capacity for focused primal insight into external reality has characterised the work of Franz Gertsch since the beginnings of his artistic recognition at the end of the 1960s right up to the present day, reaching its brilliant climax in the Seasons cycle completed in 2011.

At the same time, it is by no means self-evident that a theme as traditional as that of the seasons can hold its own in the resonance chamber of the present, and confidently refute criticism along the lines of 'distance to the problem' and 'anachronism' solely through the quality of its formulation. Quite the opposite, in fact. Because, over the centuries, music, literature and the visual arts seemed already to have said – repeatedly – everything worth saying about the change of the seasons: about its symbolic reflection of becoming, blooming and fading, about its link with human activities before industrial mass production, about its intrinsic parallelism of nature and soul space. It is precisely because of this, therefore, that the challenge facing today's working artist has increased to such an extreme degree. As if it were not enough that an artist must enter into posthumous competition with, say, Giuseppe Arcimboldo, Pieter Brueghel the Elder, Antonio Vivaldi, Joseph Haydn and all those who followed, he or she is also not spared the need to clarify the relevance of such a venture, both in the context of developing one's own oeuvre and championing it vis-à-vis a world whose natural foundations have long since been irreversibly shattered. This is a task, therefore, that requires a completely distinct, perfectly mastered range of artist's tools, as well as a human approach rooted in a rich experience of being, and an awareness of the progressive obliteration of primary realities. All these requirements are to be found to the nth degree in Franz Gertsch, yet it is no surprise that such a cycle also demands long years of internal maturation, particularly in his case. Ultimately, from the first photographs of the indigenous piece of autumn woodlands, to the unnoticed storage of the 35mm slides in the archive, to the beginning of the large-format transfer to canvas, to the concept of the seasons developed during this work, all the way to its painstaking realisation, sixteen years passed: a span of life, therefore, which primes this cycle with the patina of existential credibility, and which even at this stage assigns it something approaching the nature of a legacy.

Viewed in terms of the sequence of creation, *Summer* comes in second place after the initiating *Autumn*, and effectively forms the prelude to the programme of which we have become aware, which, after its completion, will lead to *Winter* and *Spring*. As is always the case with Gertsch, the process of rendering an original photographic motif in paint has proved to be a calculated interplay between proximity and distance, between the near-boundless wealth of detail and the demanding structure of the picture in its entirety. Proceeding from the centre of the enormous 325 x 480 centimetre surface, acrylic paint has been applied with a flat brush on unprimed cotton and 'massaged' into the body of the painting in such a way as to create a microcosm growing from one day's work to the next, which only achieves artistic wholeness at the very end. Such a process calls for immense anticipatory imaginative powers, as well as a natural disposition enabling absolute devotion to the work in progress over long periods of time, accomplished in rituals of what might be called meditative humility: in other words, a disposition demanding virtues that have become extremely rare in the 'artiness' of the present day. For Gertsch, however, these virtues have become almost trademark features, and their significant effect marks all phases of his oeuvre to date. It is found, for example, in the fascinating materiality of the hair, jumpers or denim jackets of the so-called situation portraits; it shimmers in the skin, eyes and lips of the singular facial landscapes of girls and women; and it is evident in the iridescence of the grasses, butterburs, black waters and forest paths of the late homages to nature, both painted and in woodcut. In this respect, the cycle of the Seasons – and here, in particular, *Summer* – demonstrates on the one hand the consistent updating of previous artistic intentions, and on the other the absolutely monumental sum of Gertsch's pictorial experiences. A sum, mind you, which, although due to an obsessive urge to fathom all visible realities, far transcends the visually nameable in areas where the essential questions of human conditioning have been repeatedly renegotiated since time immemorial.

Harald Kunde

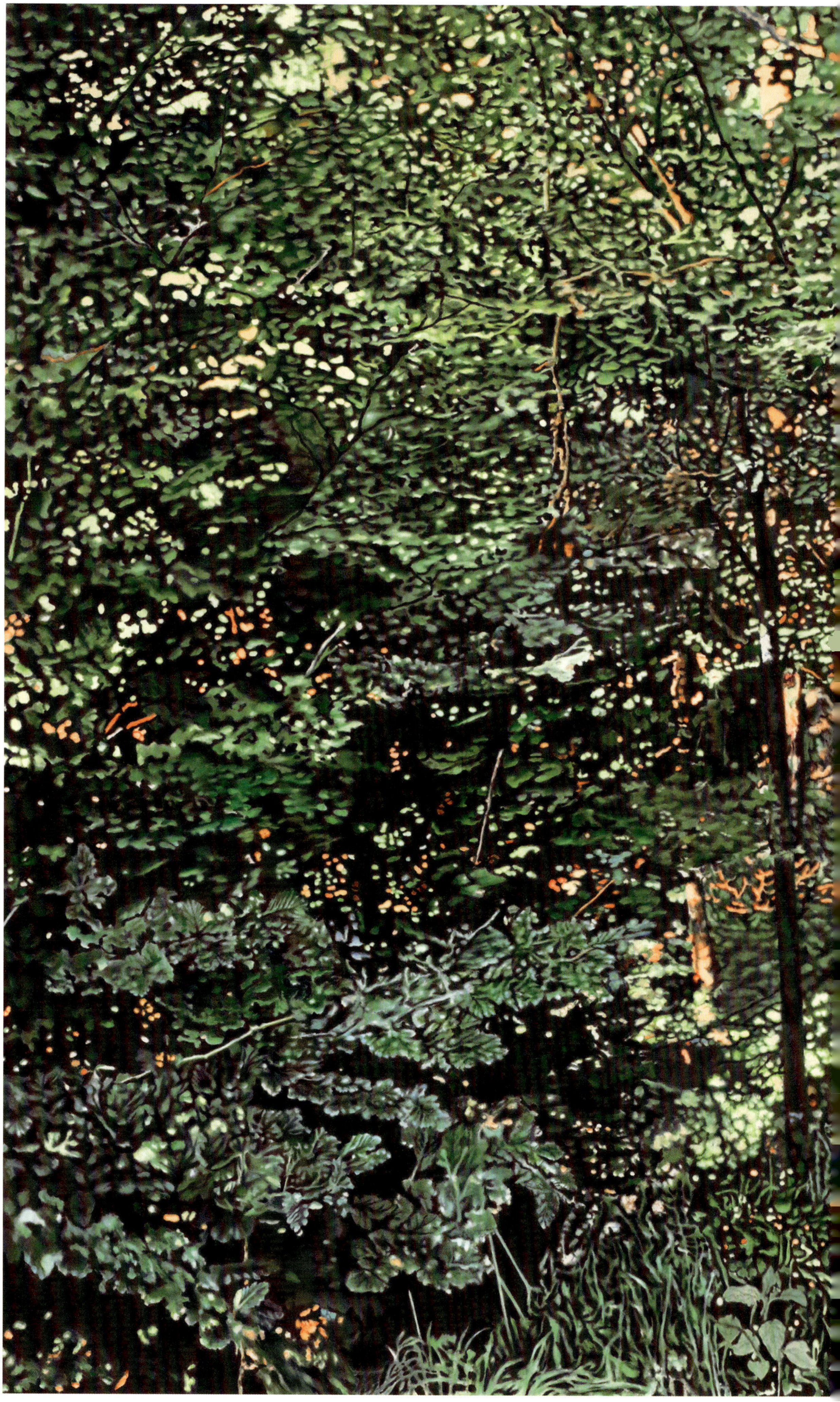

Summer, 2009
Acrylic on unprimed cotton
canvas, 325 x 480 cm
Collection of the artist

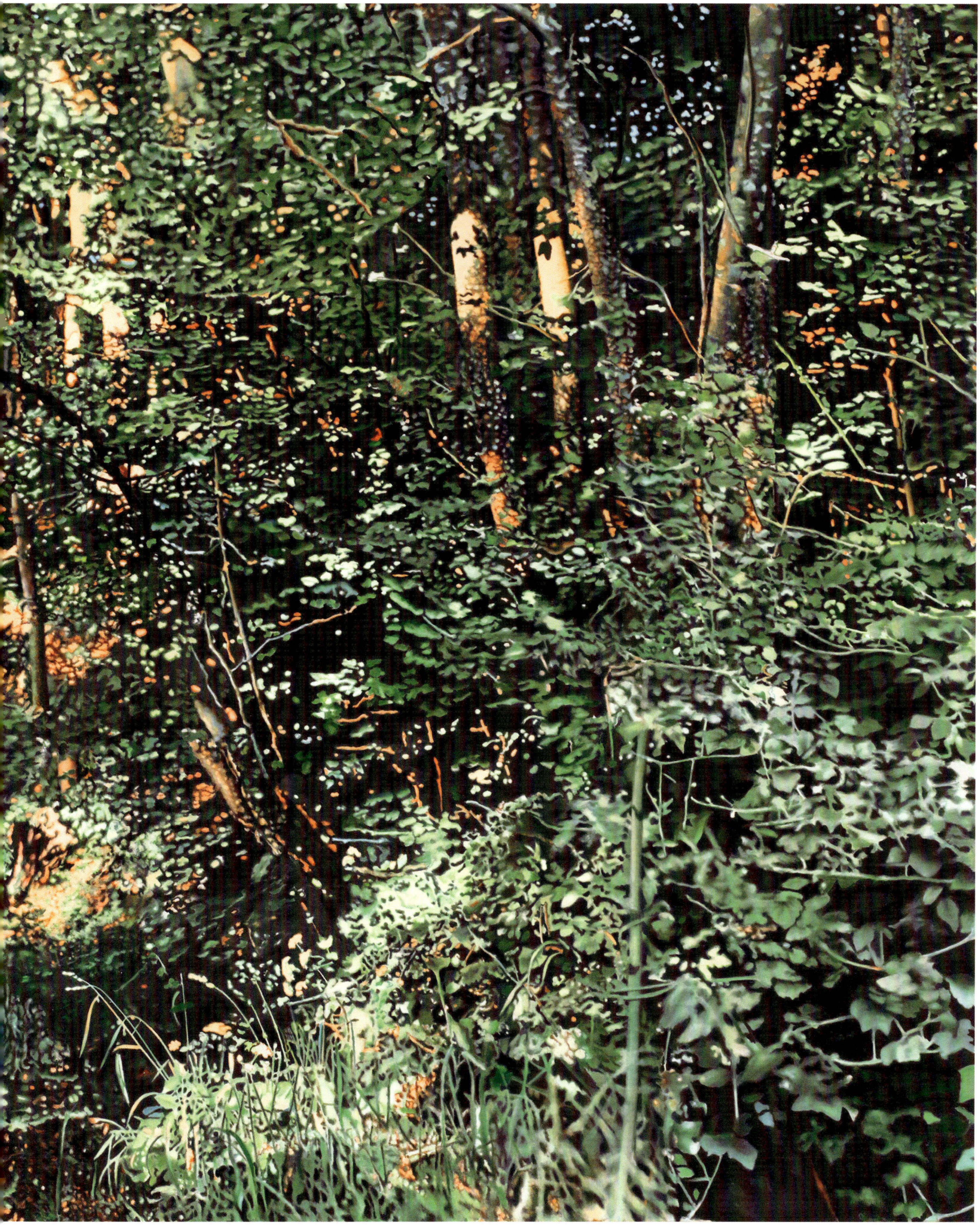

Silvia I, 1998
Egg tempera on unprimed
cotton canvas, 290 x 280 cm
museum franz gertsch, Burgdorf

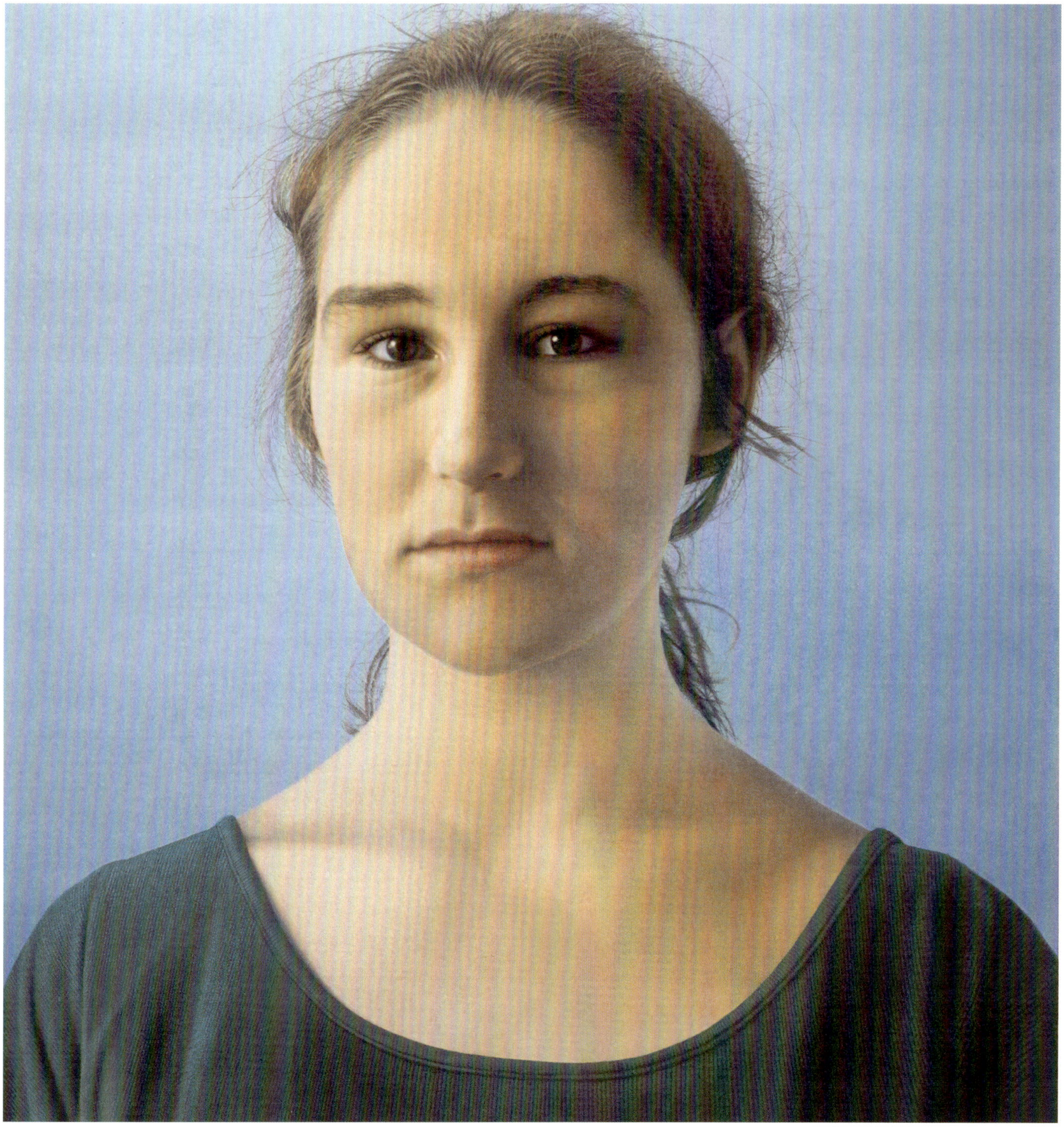

Pestwurz "Ausblick" (Butterbur 'Prospect'), 2005
Woodcut (2 plates), 268 x 183 cm each
Hand-pulled print no. 9 on Kumohadamashi Japan
paper made by Heizaburo Ivano, 276 x 380 cm
Ivory black. Collection of the artist

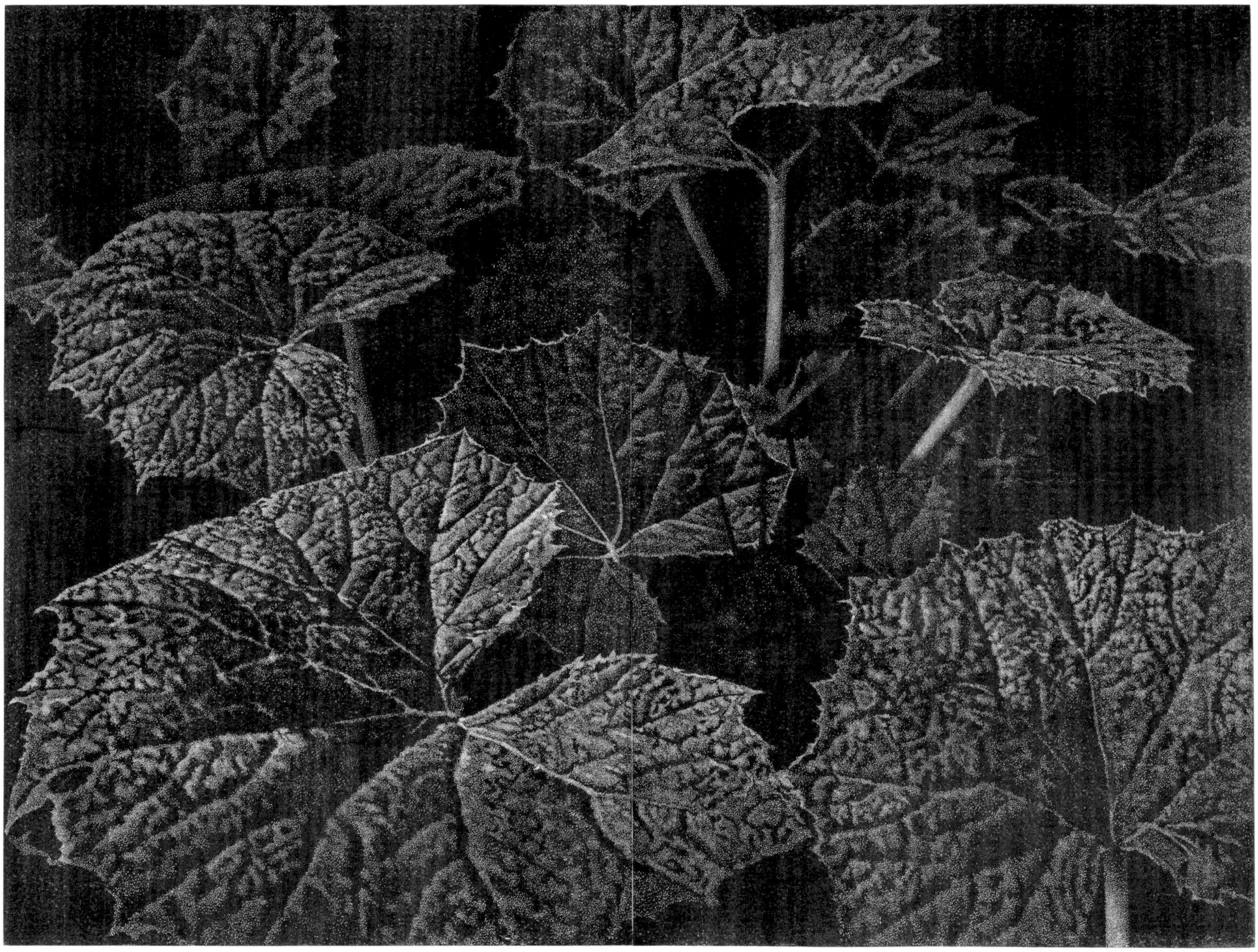

Pestwurz “Ausblick” (Butterbur ‘Prospect’), 2005
Woodcut (2 plates), 268 x 183 cm each
Hand-pulled print no. 8 on Kumohadamashi Japan
paper made by Heizaburo Ivano, 276 x 380 cm
Turquoise. Collection of the artist

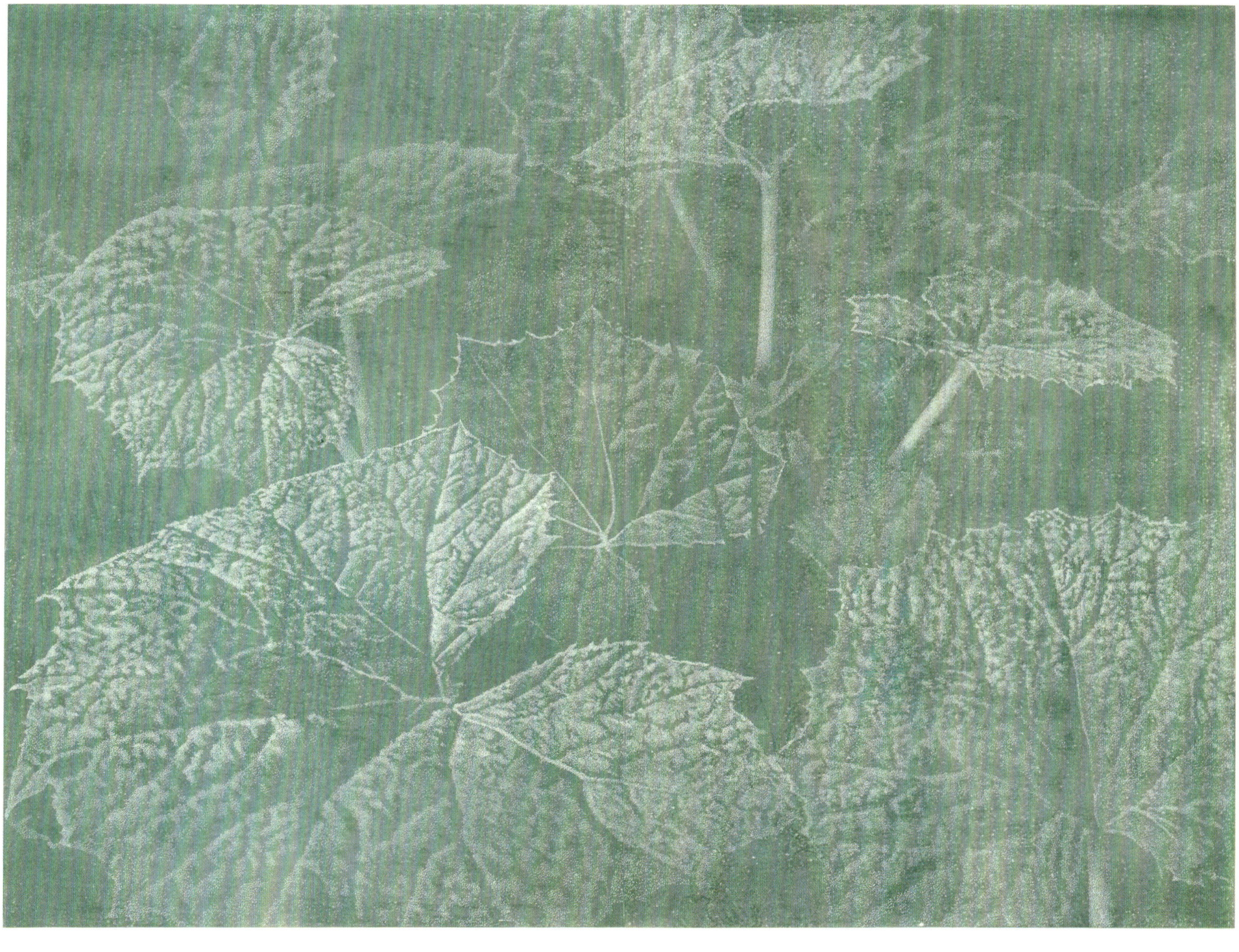

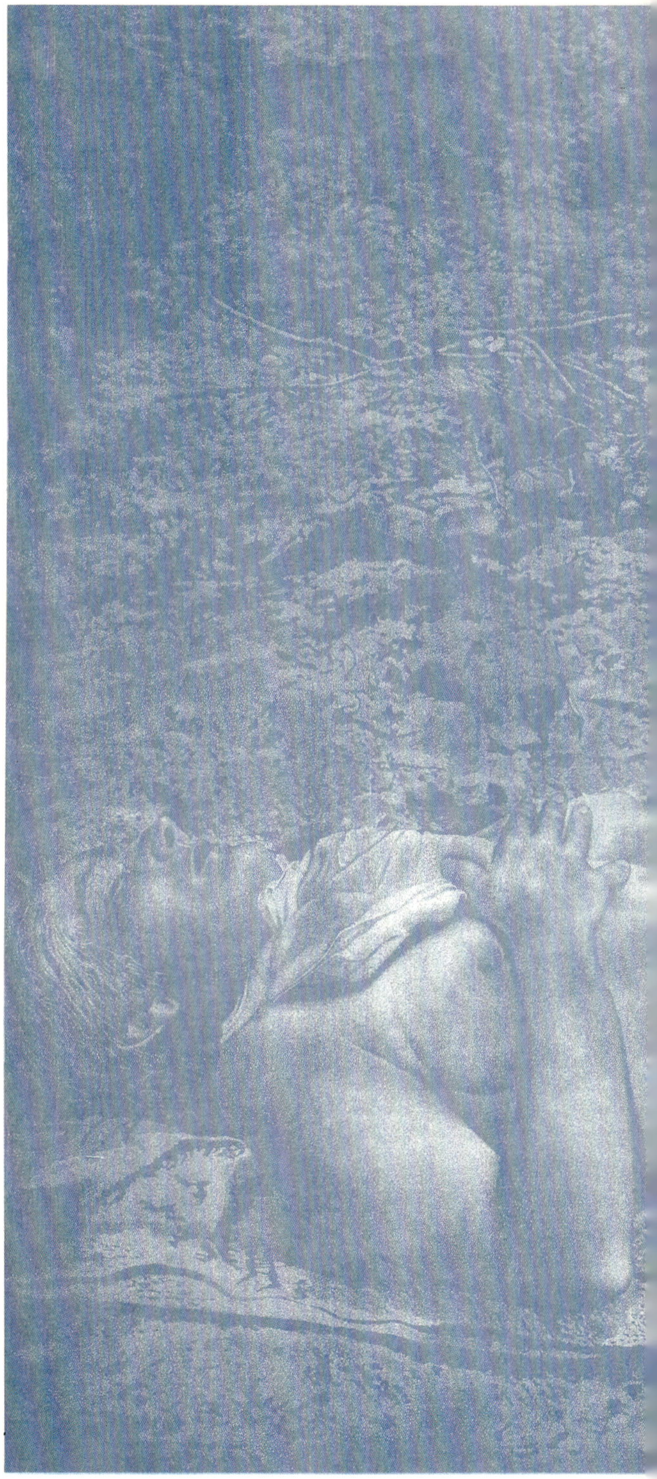

Maria, 2001
Woodcut (3 plates), 305 x 152 cm each
Hand-pulled print no. 2 on Kumohadamashi Japan
paper made by Heizaburo Ivano, 380 x 276 cm,
380 x 566 cm in total. Blue (slightly greyed)
Collection of the artist

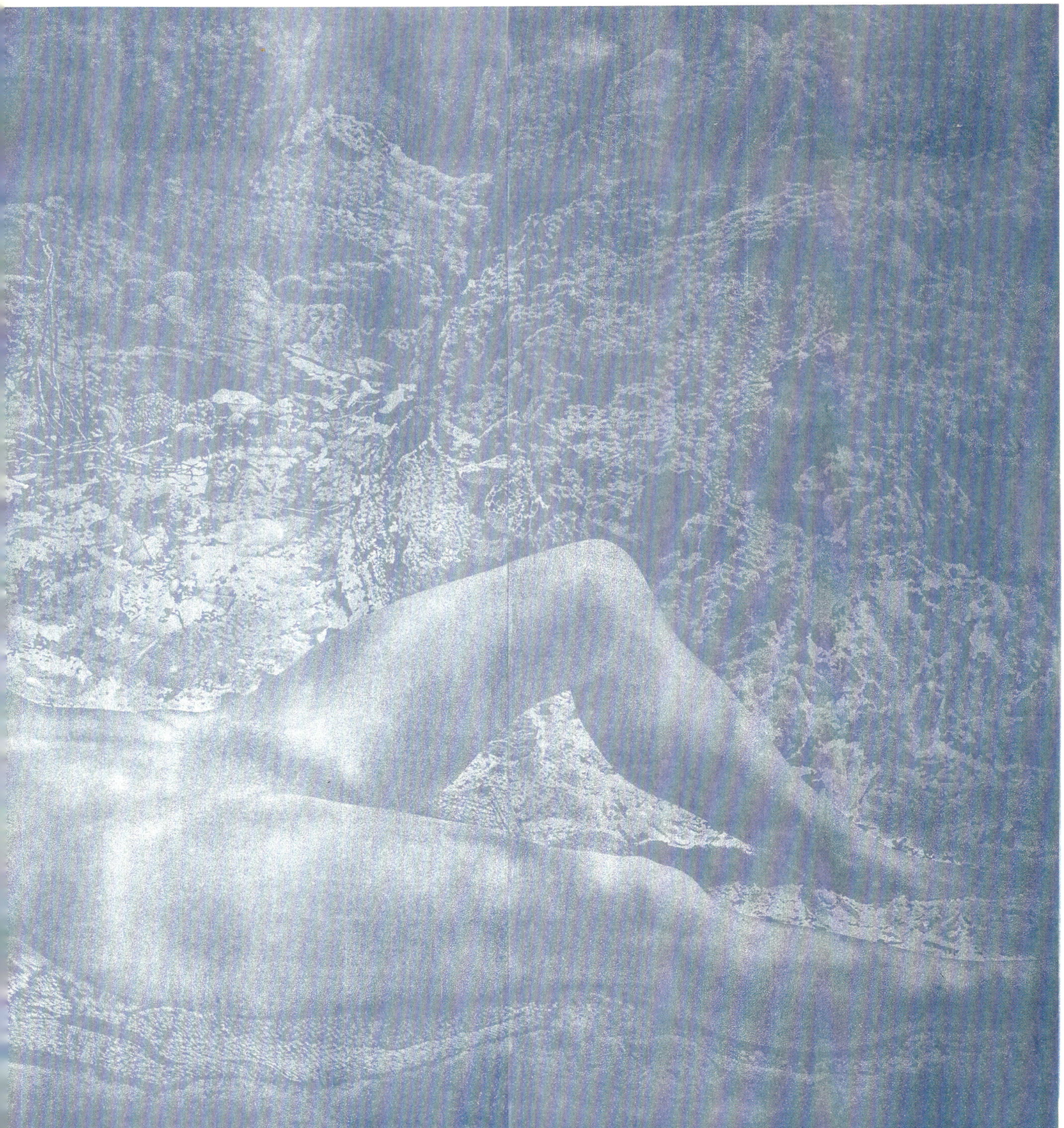

The Milky Way is
a detail
of the cosmos
The Solar System is
a detail
of the Milky Way
The Earth is
a detail
of the Solar System
Our field of vision is
a detail
of the Earth
Our forest track is
a detail
of our field of vision
and of the cosmos

Autumn is the autumn of 1994.
Summer is the summer of 2007.
Winter is the winter of 2008.
Spring is the spring of 2009.

Autumn, *Summer* and *Winter* are painted with paints I made myself (powder pigments bound with acrylic emulsion) on unprimed cotton canvas (cotton duck). Using flat, 0.5- to 1-centimetre-wide paintbrushes, the liquid paints are massaged or rubbed, so to speak, into the raw canvas, on which they combine closely with the substrate. This technique gives the paintings a velvety, matt surface, and a colour tone all of their own.

The portrait of *Spring* is an egg-tempera painting. Egg is the emulsifier that binds linseed-oil varnish and damar varnish with water. As with acrylic, the paints are paintable with water, and then dry to a waterproof finish. The difference is that acrylic paints dry waterproof very quickly, while egg-tempera paints can be solubilised for several hours longer – an advantage for this picture in terms of achieving soft colour transitions. Not even a restorer can distinguish visually between the two techniques.

Franz Gertsch, 27 February 2011

MONOGRAPHS AND CATALOGUE RAISONNÉS

Affentranger-Kirchrath, Angelika, *Franz Gertsch. Die Magie des Realen,* Wabern-Bern 2004

Ammann, Jean-Christophe, *Franz Gertsch, Träger des Kaiserrings Goslar 1997,* Goslar 1997

Beil, Ralf, *Franz Gertsch. Maria,* ed. Reinhard Spieler, Bern 2003

Franz Gertsch, ex. cat., Kunsthaus Zürich, Bern 1980 (with a complete catalogue of paintings from 1969 to 1980)

Franz Gertsch – Holzschnitte. Die Kunst liegt in der Natur. Wer sie herausreissen kann, der hat sie, with photographs by Balthasar Burkhard, Baden 1994 (published on the occasion of the exhibition *Franz Gertsch. Holzschnitte und Malerei auf Papier,* Kunstmuseum Bern and Staatliche Kunsthalle Baden-Baden 1994)

Mason, Rainer Michael, *Bois gravés monumentaux / Grossformatige Holzschnitte / Large-scale woodcuts,* Geneva, Zurich 1989 (with a complete catalogue of prints from 1972 to 1989)

museum franz gertsch. Das Buch zum Museum, Bern 2002

Ronte, Dieter, *Franz Gertsch*, with an essay by Jean-Christophe Ammann, Bern 1986 (with a complete catalogue of paintings from 1969 to 1985)

Spieler, Reinhard / Vitali, Samuel, *Franz Gertsch – Die Retrospektive*, ex. cat., museum franz gertsch, Burgdorf and Kunstmuseum Bern, 2005

BIOGRAPHY

1930 Born 8 March in Mörigen, canton of Bern, Switzerland
1947–50 Studies at Max von Mühlenen's art school, Bern
1969 First large-size realistic paintings
1970 Family and group scenes, Situations-portraits
1972 Participation at the *documenta 5*, Kassel
1976 Gertsch family moves to Rüschegg
1978 Participation at the Venice Biennale
1980 Gertsch starts painting a series of portraits with *Self-Portrait*, followed by *Irene, Tabea, Verena, Christina, Johanna*
1986 Gertsch stops painting and concentrates on large-scale woodcuts
1994 Starts painting again; up to 1999 *Gräser I–IV* and *Silvia* (1997/98) are created
1997 Wins the 'Kaiserring' Goslar Award for Modern Art
1999 Solo show at the Venice Biennale
2002 Opening of the museum franz gertsch in Burgdorf/CH
2005 Retrospective at the museum franz gertsch and the Kunstmuseum Bern; successive venues for the exhibition are Aachen, Tübingen and Vienna (2006)
2007 Starts painting the cycle of the four seasons with *Herbst [Autumn]* (2008) followed by *Sommer [Summer]* (2009) and *Winter* (2009)
2011 Completion of *Frühling [Spring]*

SELECTED SOLO EXHIBITIONS

2011 *Franz Gertsch. Seasons. Works 1983 to 2011*, Kunsthaus Zürich

2006 *Franz Gertsch. Retrospektive – das malerische Werk 1951–1984*, MUMOK Museum für Moderne Kunst Stiftung Ludwig, Vienna, in conjunction with
Franz Gertsch. Naturporträts, Albertina, Vienna

2005 *Franz Gertsch. Die Retrospektive*, museum franz gertsch, Burgdorf, Kunstmuseum Bern, Ludwig Forum für Internationale Kunst, Aachen (2006), Kunsthalle Tübingen (2006)

2004 *Franz Gertsch – Patti Smith*, Gagosian Gallery, New York

2003 *Franz Gertsch. Silvia*, kestnergesellschaft, Hannover
Franz Gertsch – Patti Smith, museum franz gertsch, Burgdorf, Pinakothek der Moderne, Munich

2002 *Franz Gertsch. Das Gesamtwerk 1987–2002*, opening exhibition at museum franz gertsch, Burgdorf
Franz Gertsch. Monumentale Holzschnitte, Bündner Kunstmuseum, Chur

1999 *Franz Gertsch – Gemälde und Holzschnitte 1987 bis 1997*, Museum Kurhaus Kleve

1997 *Franz Gertsch – Landschaften und Porträts 1986–1995*, Hamburger Bahnhof – Museum für Gegenwart, Staatliche Museen zu Berlin
Franz Gertsch, Cabinet des estampes, Musée d'art et d'histoire, Geneva

1995 *Franz Gertsch*, Aichi Prefectural Museum of Art, Nagoya

1994 *Franz Gertsch. Holzschnitte 1986–1994*, Staatliche Kunsthalle Baden-Baden
Franz Gertsch. Holzschnitte und Malerei auf Papier, Kunstmuseum Bern

1993 *Franz Gertsch. Landschaften*, Graphische Sammlung der ETH, Zürich, Städtische Galerie im Städelschen Kunstinstitut, Frankfurt a. M.

1991 *Franz Gertsch. Holzschnitte*, Städtische Galerie im Lenbachhaus, Munich

Franz Gertsch. Nine Large Scale Woodcuts, Hirshhorn Museum and Sculpture Garden, Washington, D.C., San Jose Museum of Art

1990 *Franz Gertsch. Large Scale Woodcuts*, series 'Projects', Museum of Modern Art, New York

1989 *Franz Gertsch. Bois gravés monumentaux. Grossformatige Holzschnitte. Large-scale woodcuts*, Cabinet des estampes und Musée Rath, Musée d'art et d'histoire, Geneva

1986 *Franz Gertsch*, Museum Moderner Kunst, Vienna, Kunsthalle Basel

1980 *Franz Gertsch*, Kunsthaus Zürich, Sprengel Museum Hannover

1975 *Franz Gertsch*, Akademie der Künste, Berlin, Kunstverein Braunschweig, Kunsthalle Düsseldorf, Kunsthalle Basel

1973 *Franz Gertsch*, Nancy Hoffmann Gallery, New York

1972 *Franz Gertsch*, Galerie Mikro, Berlin

IMPRINT

This book is published on the occasion of the exhibition
Franz Gertsch. Seasons – Works 1983 to 2011
Kunsthaus Zürich 10 June – 18 September 2011

Exhibition:
Curator *Tobia Bezzola*
Project coordination *Sandra Haldi*
Conservation *Hanspeter Marty*
Art Handling *Robert Sulzer & team*
Insurance/Transport *Gerda Kram*
Documentation *Cécile Brunner*
Public Relations *Björn Quellenberg, Kristin Steiner*
Sponsorship *Monique Spaeti*

Catalogue:
Editor *Zürcher Kunstgesellschaft/Kunsthaus Zürich*
Editing *Tobia Bezzola, Sandra Haldi*
Translations *Debbie Nichol*
Project Management Kerber Verlag *Katrin Günther*
Copyediting *Sarah Quigley*
Graphic Design *Franziska Schott & Marco Schibig,* Bern

The Deutsche Nationalbibliothek lists this publication in the Deutsche Nationalbibliografie; detailed bibliographic data is available on the Internet at http://dnb.d-nb.de.

Printed and published by:
Kerber Verlag, Bielefeld
Windelsbleicher Str. 166–170
33659 Bielefeld, Germany
Tel. +49 (0) 5 21/9 50 08-10
Fax +49 (0) 5 21/9 50 08-88
info@kerberverlag.com
www.kerberverlag.com

Kerber, US Distribution
D.A.P., Distributed Art Publishers, Inc.
New York, NY 10013
Tel. +1 212 6 27 19 99
Fax +1 212 6 27 94 84

KERBER publications are available in selected bookshops worldwide (distributed in Europe, Asia, South and North America).

This work is protected by copyright in whole and in part. The reproduction or communication of this work in any form or by any means without prior permission from the publisher is illegal and punishable. This applies to all acts of use, in particular such as the reproduction of texts and pictures, their performance and demonstration, translation, filming, microfilming, broadcasting, storage and processing in electronic media. Infringements will be punishable by prosecution.

© 2011 Credits, text illustrations:
Balthasar Burkhard archive (pp. 48/49), Matthias Baus, Köln (pp. 20/21), Beat Jost, Bern (pp. 15, 17, 44, 61), Günther Kathrein, Zürich (pp. 65, 69), Jochen Littkemann, Berlin (pp. 31, 35, 37), Dominique Uldry (pp. 13, 19, 26/27, 29, 33, 42/43, 47, 51, 58/59, 63, 67, 74/75, 77, 79, 81, 82/83)
In the case of any individual copyright holders with own legal rights not being cited by name, please contact the editors.

Cover illustration: Franz Gertsch, *Winter,* 2009

© 2011 Franz Gertsch
© 2011 Zürcher Kunstgesellschaft/Kunsthaus Zürich,
Kerber Verlag, Bielefeld/Leipzig/Berlin
© 2011 for the texts by the authors

ISBN 978-3-86678-520-5

Printed in Germany

Swiss Re

Partner for contemporary art